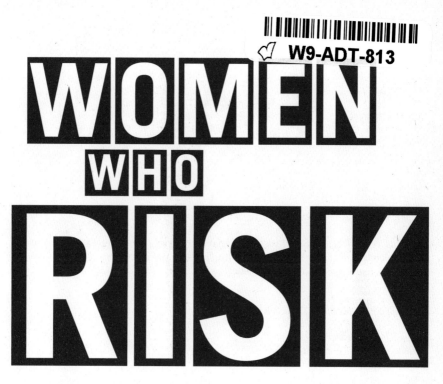

WOMEN WHO RISK

Profiles of Women in Extreme Sports

Marilyn Olsen

HATHERLEIGH PRESS
NEW YORK, NY

Photo credits:

Indianapolis Motor Speedway	back cover right, pp. 4, 7
Beth Wald	front cover, p. 63
Jeff Schultz	pp. 74, 83
Doug Ogden	pp, 115, 116
Peter Brouillet	back cover left, 129
Keoki Flagg	p. 179

FIRST PAPERBACK EDITION 2003

A Healthy Living Book
Published by Hatherleigh Press
5-22 46th Avenue, Suite 200
Long Island City, NY 11101
Toll Free 1-800-528-2550
Visit our Web sites healthylivingbooks.com and hatherleighpress.com

Hatherleigh Press books are available for bulk purchase, special promotions and premiums. For more information on reselling and special purchase opportunities, please call us at 1-800-528-2550 and ask for the Special Sales Manager.

Library of Congress Cataloging-in-Publication Data

Olsen, Marilyn.
       Women who risk / Marilyn Olsen.
               p. cm.
       ISBN 1-57826-124-4 (alk. paper)
          1. Women athletes—United States—Biography. 2. Extreme sports—United States. I. Title.

   GV697.A1 O42 2001
   796'.082'092273—dc21
   [B]

                                                                    2001039073

Cover Design by Corin Hirsch
Interior Design by Angel Harleycat

10 9 8 7 6 5 4 3 2 1
Printed in Canada on acid-free paper.

Table of Contents

Introduction

Extreme sports have always been a strictly spectator activity for me. When I was growing up, girls didn't play sports. Although the house I grew up in was across the street from Lake Michigan, we girls didn't swim. We sat on the beach or went sailing. In my high school, physical education consisted of playing badminton or girl's basketball—a half court game where you could dribble the ball only twice before you had to pass it to someone else. In that game it was nearly impossible to even work up a sweat.

I didn't learn to ski until I was an adult and even today my children describe my performance on the slopes more in terms of its comedic value than as an athletic endeavor. The most extreme thing I ever did athletically was walk a Leukemia Society benefit marathon from Big Sur to Carmel. During the many hours it took me to finish, my primary accomplishment was getting to see the backs of just about everybody else in the race.

So, as I started writing this book, it was with a sense of awe. I had seen these women do the things they did and I didn't think I'd ever be able to understand how or why they did them. Now I do.

It goes without saying that the eleven women whose stories are included in *Women Who Risk* are all truly amazing. They have done, and continue to do things every day that most of us will never be able to do even once in our whole lives. They are all superb athletes and admirable human beings. It was a great honor to get to know them.

Not surprisingly, I found that they have much in common. They are all extremely disciplined people. They set ambitious goals and do what it takes to reach them. They are intensely focused. Many have had to overcome many obstacles to reach the high goals they have set for themselves. All have done whatever it took—working second and third jobs, making personal sacrifices—to be the best of the best in their chosen sport.

That's not to say they're all alike. They range in age from 20 to mid 40s. Some became involved in their sport as small children—others not until they were in their 20s or 30s. Five of the women are professionals in their sports. One is a semi-pro, three are amateurs, one is an instructor, and one is essentially retired from her sport. One of the women is a single working mother with two children. Two are also authors. Several are extremely entrepreneurial, others work for giant corporations. Some of them have been featured in the national media and have become well-known celebrities. Others do what they do simply for the personal satisfaction it brings.

While these women have distinctly different personalities, some voluble and easy to talk to, others more introspective, all were gracious and willing to share their stories, thoughts and dreams. It is obvious that they care deeply about what they do and are anxious to help others understand.

There is also considerable generosity in each of these women. Certainly the contracts of some of the professionals require that they make public appearances and sign autographs, but above and beyond that I found that all were sincerely interested in helping younger women in their sport persevere and become successful.

I can't say that I have come to know these women well, but I can say with certainty, that what I do know of them I like very much. Women who risk are women who are to be admired. They are pioneers, exceptional examples, women who should inspire all of us to be all that we can be.

—*Marilyn Olsen*

1

Let the Race Come to You

A Profile of Sarah Fisher—Auto Racer

Of all the auto racing tracks around the world, none is perhaps more famous than the Indianapolis Motor Speedway, where the annual running of the Indianapolis 500 has long been known as The Greatest Spectacle in Racing. Constructed in the spring of 1909, the original track featured 3.2 million bricks. Although asphalt now covers most of them, a 36-inch- wide strip of bricks still designates the start-finish line and the track is still affectionately called The Brickyard.

The first Indianapolis 500 was held in 1911; it was won by Ray Harroun, with an average speed of 74.602 mph. Now cars regularly achieve speeds in excess of 220 mph and champions have raced into Victory Lane every year except the war years of 1917-18 and 1942-45.

In 1994, Indianapolis Motor Speedway owner Tony George (grandson of Tony Hulman, who had owned the track since the 1940s) announced the formation of the Indy Racing League (IRL), challenging Championship Auto Racing Teams (CART) that had dominated racing at Indianapolis since 1980. In founding the IRL, George hoped to make open wheel racing more affordable and encourage younger and less experienced drivers to compete. To accomplish this goal, in 1995, George ruled that 25 of the 33 positions at the 1996 race would be reserved for the top 25 drivers in the IRL standings. CART retaliated by scheduling a race at the Michigan International Raceway, timed to directly compete with the Indy 500. By 2000, however, relations between the two leagues had improved somewhat and some CART owners have begun to return to the race.

For the first 84 races, the Indy 500 was strictly a male event. It wasn't until 1984 that Janet Guthrie became the first woman to drive in the race, followed more than 10 years later by Lyn St. James in 1997. In 2000, Sarah Fisher became the third.

Guthrie and St. James arrived at the Indy 500 late in their racing careers (St. James was 52). Sarah, at age 19, was not only the third woman to enter the race, she was also the youngest driver ever to compete. A collision, ironically with the only other woman in the race, Lyn St. James, dashed Sarah's hopes of a rookie win, but not her desire to take the checkered flag in years to come.

* * *

Dressed in brown corduroy pants, a navy blue crew neck sweater and a bluish green baseball cap, Sarah Fisher sits at a desk in Indianapolis staring intently at the detailed computerized image of a steering wheel. It's not the image millions of Sarah Fisher's fans around the world probably have of her. They're much more familiar with the Sarah Fisher standing on the podium at the Texas Motor Speedway clutching a trophy and a bottle of champagne. The Sarah Fisher leaning over the pit wall in Phoenix to sign autographs. The Sarah Fisher roaring around the track at the Indianapolis 500 at more than 200 miles per hour. But it is just as real a picture of Sarah Fisher as the glossy photographs on the front pages of newspapers and magazines or the petite, soft spoken young

At age 19, Sarah Fisher became the youngest person and third woman ever to race in the Indianapolis 500.

woman patiently answering the same questions over and over again on ESPN. This Sarah Fisher is the everyday Sarah Fisher, a working member of a team of forty or so people at Walker Racing, whose goal it is to put together all the pieces it takes to win in one of the highest stakes sports there is.

None of this is new to Sarah Fisher now, not the celebrity, the cheering fans, the endless interviews or, certainly, the hard work behind the scenes. Although she just turned 20 in October 2000, she has been racing, answering questions and trying to solve complicated engineering problems for more than fifteen years.

Before most kids her age could spell the word car, Sarah's parents put her behind the wheel of one. To the surprise and delight of David and Reba Fisher, who had met while both were racing, their little girl, age five, seemed to have inherited both the skill and enthusiasm to excel in the family sport. While her first grade friends had yet to learn to ride a bicycle, Sarah was competing in quarter midgets in every race the family could find around central Ohio.

"My mom tried to get me interested in other things like playing the piano, soccer and swimming," says Sarah," but, even then, I was an independent sort of person and I just always liked racing more."

A couple of years in the quarter midgets gave Sarah enough experience in steering and using simple controls that by the time she was eight she'd graduated to go-karts. At least 20 times a year, the family loaded up the kart and all the gear that went with it and traveled to races from New York to Florida and from Virginia back to Ohio. Enthusiasm quickly turned to excellence. Between the ages of 11 and 14, Sarah took the World Karting Association Grand National Championship three times and, in 1993, was the Circleville Points Champion.

At age 15, when most of the girl athletes her age were playing school or club sports like soccer, softball or basketball, Sarah moved up to sprint cars. "This was a big step up for me," says Sarah. "These are powerful cars with a V-8, 800-horsepower engine on a 1,200 pound chassis. This is a huge engine for such a light weight vehicle." For the first time, Sarah had to learn to cope with wings and down forces and a variety of track surfaces and configurations.

The change in cars brought with it what even Sarah describes as a brutal schedule. "With the sprints, we'd go to about 60 races a year. Because we owned the cars, we'd not only race but have to do all the maintenance. Since we were on a dirt track, after each race we'd have to thoroughly wash the car. Because washing would take off all the grease, we'd have to grease it up all over again. We didn't have anyone to help with all of this. It was just my dad and me. So we'd race, then we'd work on the car, then we'd load everything up and head off to another race the next day. During those years, we traveled from Pennsylvania to Oklahoma and from Florida to Texas. I'd take my school homework with me and after we'd finally get settled someplace, I'd hit the books. Whenever I think I have a busy schedule now, I think back over the three years we did that."

At age 18, Sarah made another change, this time to midgets, traveling the North American Midget Auto Racing Series (NAMARS) on asphalt ovals, winning five of the 23 races she entered. Meanwhile, she graduated from Teays Valley High School in Commercial Point, Ohio with a GPA of more than 4.1 on a 4.0 scale, having somehow found time to take honors level classes.

At age 19, she moved up again, this time to Indy cars. In 1999 Sarah became the youngest person to pass the Indy Racing League rookie test at the Las Vegas Motor Speedway. She started fifth at the Midas 500 classic, setting a record for the highest starting position by a woman.

Enter Derrick Walker. By 1999, Walker had become one of the most respected names in Indy car history. A native of Scotland, who started his racing career as a mechanic, Walker had three Formula One wins, 28 CART (Championship Auto Racing Team) wins and five Indianapolis 500 wins as well as having been general manager, team manager and vice president of Penske Racing for 13 years. In 1990, he had started his own team, Walker Racing, headquartered just a few miles from the Indianapolis Motor Speedway.

When Tony George, owner of the Indianapolis Motor Speedway, announced the creation of the IRL in 1995, Walker, who still also races in the CART series, made the decision to find a driver to compete in the IRL, as well. "He called me before that first race in Texas," says Sarah. She signed with him on January 18, 2000. One of the stipulations of the contract was that, for the first time, Sarah's dad would not have an active role in her career.

Around the same time, Sarah had made the decision to start her college education at Butler University. The combination of the Walker Racing contract and college enrollment meant a move to Indianapolis.

"That was a big change for me," says Sarah. "I'm an only child and through racing had spent a lot more time with my parents than other kids do. But it was definitely for the best. This is a very serious business. It's a huge dollar sport. If you get your family involved, you can't communicate the way you need to. It would never have worked to have had my dad as crew chief."

Starting college at the same time she was beginning a professional career in an extremely demanding sport was also a major decision, but typical of the pragmatic approach Sarah has taken to most decisions in her life.

"I'd certainly been through the college of racing, but I felt that it was important for me to get my college degree and get it fairly soon. Racing is obviously a very big part of my life, but as a driver, I know that anything can happen, anytime.

I've always been interested in the engineering side of racing, so a degree in mechanical engineering will give me the credentials to stay in racing long after I will probably still be a driver."

Although Walker could have attracted any number of established drivers to his IRL team, "I thought since I was starting in a new league it might make sense to start with a rookie. Kent Liffick, one of the IRL's promotions staff members suggested that I take a look at Sarah. At that time I didn't know anything about her, but I found out quite soon what a gifted girl she was in the sprint circuit."

Even though Walker was a prominent name in the racing community, signing Sarah was, in his words, "a big commitment," he says. "At first I didn't think I would have the resources to build a program around a whole series. Many people thought that having a girl driver would be such a novelty that it would be easy to get sponsors. But I've been around this sport long enough to know that you have to be a driver first. There's too much at stake for men to be willing to make concessions to a driver just because she's a girl. All the teams are selling racing. I knew that if she couldn't drive, I might just as well set fire to my money."

In signing Sarah, Walker also took the risk involved in signing someone who was barely out of her teens.

"Taking on a very young driver is a big responsibility," says Walker. "There is a lot required to build a young talent. But, on the other hand, you have a chance to mold them. Your hope is that the young driver will grow with you, eventually retire with you. The advantage is that a young driver like Sarah is still pure, there's no chip on her shoulder, she doesn't have an attitude. Plus, she's a smart kid. I know she's going to have a lot of questions about what we do. That's OK. That's how she'll learn. We're in this together. Sarah has a great personality. She's like the girl next door. Yet she knows how to talk and has the education outside racing. When I signed her, I thought the only thing she was missing was time on the track. We can give her that. I gave her a five-year contract having never seen her drive. That might be the dumbest or smartest thing I've ever done."

Another consideration for Sarah and Walker was the lack of a major sponsor. "Sponsorship is a huge issue in auto racing since racing is such a very expensive sport," says Sarah. "Unless the driver brings money to the team, like some foreign drivers do, you have to be given the chance to prove yourself so that the sponsors will come to you. Unlike some other drivers, I couldn't go to a team and say, 'Hey, here's $3 million. Let's go racing.' Yet, I am beginning to understand that it is money that ultimately keeps you racing. If you're on a tighter budget, you're always having to make choices."

"My philosophy is that you focus first on what works," says Walker. "When you're a success, sponsors will be falling out of the trees."

Although drivers and racing teams are seen by the public as part of one big organization, most drivers like Sarah are independent contractors. "I'm an employee of Sarah Fisher, LLC," says Sarah. "I do what the contract says."

Within the last year, that has included a lot of things that aren't related to the car or her driving.

"I'm obligated to make a lot of public appearances," says Sarah. "I've been to New York to talk to some marketing groups, to Chicago to sign autographs and been on the radio a lot. At first it worried me that all this publicity stuff was taking up such a large percentage of my time. Over time, though, I've warmed up to it. It gets easier as you go along. You get asked the same questions over and over again, so it's not hard to come up with an answer."

"Getting into the IRL was a huge transition from sprints," says Sarah. "Probably the hardest part of races like the Indy 500 for me is the patience it requires. I'm so used to short tracks. When you're out there for 500 miles, there's a whole lot more time for stuff to happen. It's easy to get distracted or upset with something that shouldn't have happened. You have to keep saying to yourself that you have a race to win and that's all that's important. You have to let the race come to you."

Another transition was the role Sarah plays as part of the team. "Before this year, I was used to being very hands-on. For all those years, my dad and I had done all of the work on the cars. At this level, though, you have to let go of that. This is a really big business with a lot of money riding on what you do. Everyone on that team has a specific job to do and you have to concentrate on doing yours and not second-guessing theirs. Once I got to know these guys, it was easier than I thought it would be."

Although Sarah no longer works on the car herself, she still has a lot of input into how the car is designed. Driving is only one of her responsibilities at Walker Racing. During the off season, her contract calls for her to be a part of the engineering team, studying the design of the car, producing working drawings.

"You have to know your car and know your engineer," says Sarah. "The longer you stay together the more you can read each other's mind. I think I had a real advantage in this since after all those years of racing with my dad, who was a mechanical engineer, I was used to discussing the car and how it was handling."

"You're never really the only one out there," says Sarah. "It takes a whole fleet of people to run a race like this. I may not actually do a lot of the jobs I used to, but I think it's important that I understand exactly what's going on."

"One of her major assets is that she knows and is interested in how the car works," says Walker. "She's like Rick Mears in that way. He drives with his head. He feels what the car is doing all the time."

Unlike the cars Sarah drove as a kid, the Indy car she drives now is incredibly complex and incredibly expensive. The chassis of the #15 Cummins Special Dallara Oldsmobile cost Walker racing $290,000. The engine another $100,000. Although it may be a good deal less elaborate than Formula One cars that can cost in the millions of dollars, still it is a mechanical and aerodynamic marvel. Weighing just 1,550 pounds, it has 650 horsepower and a top speed of 230 mph. The wheel base is 126 inches and it is 78 inches wide and 196 inches long. It can carry about 35 gallons of methanol and gets a whopping 1.85 miles per gallon.

On the outside, the car is custom made to comply with IRL specifications. Inside it is custom—made for Sarah. The exterior or "tub" is composed of a carbon fiber composite that is designed to be light and to absorb the majority of the impact if the car crashes into the wall or another car. The inside of the car is lined with a special fire-resistant foam, molded to Sarah's body to give it support and keep her as comfortable as possible throughout the race. "At these speeds, you just can't be distracted by anything," says Sarah.

"If you're not comfortable, that's going to be a distraction."

Everything in the car is fireproof or fire resistant. Driving shoes have a fire retardant lining and fire retardant gloves offer enough protection to give her time to unfasten harnesses and seat belts in the event of a fire, but are not so bulky that she can't flex her fingers. She also wears a balaclava, fire resistant underwear and an outer coverall. Her helmet is made of fiberglass, Kevlar and carbon fiber.

Woven through the interior of the car is a maze of wiring that provides Sarah with the ability to communicate with her team. Fifteen channels give the team back in the pits details about how the car is performing at all times.

"Communication is a major factor in Indy car racing," says Sarah. "When I'm in the car with my helmet on and the headrests in place, I really can't see much of anything that's around me. I have to rely a lot on the two people on the radio. One of them is the spotter on the roof, the other is the chief engineer. The spotter can see where all the cars are and his job is to tell you where you are in relation to other cars by giving you information like 'car high,' or 'car low.' The chief engineer sits in the pits and is constantly asking you what adjustments you think you might want to make. He's also the one who tells you when to pit. You have to get used to people talking to you like God all the time."

"It's very unusual that a 20-year-old would be able to cope with all that talk during the race, but Sarah can," says Walker. "She really has a feel for the car."

"For the Indy 500, I promoted myself to chief spotter," says Walker. I knew that she trusted me and that I was behind her 100%. My job was to keep her aware of the big picture, to keep her focused on what had to happen at each point toward that goal. There's so much going on during a race. One of the jobs of the team is to shield the driver from overload."

"Racing at this level is more of a thinking game," says Sarah. "I can see readouts of all of the telemetry in the car, but I don't pay much attention to them. I don't want to be distracted by thinking about all of that while I'm trying to concentrate on driving. You have to focus completely and pay attention to what you're doing."

Although to the average fan, racecars appear to be pretty much alike, in truth each is unique. Because they are so light and have so much horsepower, cars that go this fast must have wings attached to both the front and the back of the car. The wings work like an airplane wing, only in reverse. Whereas an airplane wing is designed to allow the plane to lift off the ground, the wings on a racecar are designed to push it onto the ground and, as much as possible, keep the tires in contact with the surface of the track. Since keeping the tires in contact with the track as much as possible is imperative to maintaining speed, it is vital that the car be in balance. So in all racecars there are a number of weights distributed around the car. How these weights and the wings are placed and adjusted prior to and during the race is known as the car's "set up."

"The engineering of the car is so complicated," says Walker. "On any day, there are probably 50 different ways to set that car up. You always have multiple choices as to what to do."

"Because each track is different, how your car is engineered and how you drive your car has to change with every race, too," says Sarah. "That's what really attracts me to racing. When you play ball sports, for example, although you may be on a field or a court in a different city, essentially, you're still playing in the same place. The fields and courts are all alike. In auto racing every race is a new puzzle. The Indianapolis 500 is a 2.5 mile oval and has four distinct corners whereas the Texas track has more like two corners and two bends in the straightaway. You have to be ready for that. It also makes a tremendous difference what the pavement is like, whether it is old or new and how the track is banked."

Like most other athletes, Sarah finds that practice is one thing, competition something else entirely. "What you can do on a track is a lot different when you're out there alone during practice or qualifications as opposed to when there are thirty or more drivers around you all competing for the same space."

"Being a rookie is also a disadvantage. Most of the people I compete against have experience on these tracks that I don't. So I have two problems —learning how to handle the car on that track and going fast. The other guys only have one problem—going fast."

"In this sport, you can never go too fast," says Walker. "That's what it's all about."

In addition to practice, competing in the upper ranks of auto racing demands considerable physical strength.

"Strength training is really important in this sport," says Sarah. "When most people think of driving, even for long distances, they may think, well, how hard could that be? But this is different. In a race car, you're wedged tight into that cockpit and you'll be there for 500 miles going almost 200 miles an hour or more for at least two and a half hours. You're under a lot of pressure, both mentally and physically. Mentally, there's the fact that when you're in that car, you have to pay attention every minute. In this sport, a tiny mistake can send you spinning into the wall at 200 mph or crashing into someone else at that speed and wrecking a quarter of a million dollar car.

"Then there's the design of the car. Because of the wings and under trays and other aerodynamic features, there are tremendous g-forces at work. The best way I can describe the feeling is that it's like what you feel in a commercial jet as it's taking off. Your body is literally pressed into that seat. That's what this is like all the time you're in the car. You're up against tremendous pressure with any movement you make with your arms or your legs or feet. These cars are designed so that if you got up to speed, you could literally stick to the ceiling. You have to have the strength to resist all that pressure. Also, you can't ever think about being tired. If your arm hurts or you get a cramp in your leg and you start thinking about that, you'll lose focus and make a big mistake."

To be in shape for the beating a race car driver's body takes, Sarah follows a strict training program. "Every morning I try to be at the gym from 8:00 a.m. to 10:00 a.m.," she says. "I also do a lot of cardio exercises five times a week. I love to swim. I do that a lot because it's easy on the joints. But I also run, bike and roller blade, too.

Diet is another consideration.

"I'm trying to be better about what I eat," says Sarah. "My contract with Walker Racing states right there that I have to be physically fit. I'll admit that it's hard to get over wanting the food I ate as a teenager. But I know that now that I'm 20, my metabolism will change and that all that junk food won't work anymore. I've been paying a lot more attention to getting the right balance of proteins and carbohydrates, fruits, vegetables and juice and I try to eat more chicken than beef. I don't do the Twinkie things anymore and I'm trying to stay away from sugar as much as possible."

Time management is another skill Sarah finds a necessity. "When I'm not in school, I go work out, then I come to the shop, do interviews and work on engineering. When I'm in school, I have to change that routine a little. I may have to go to class in the morning, work at the shop in the afternoon and then go to the gym at night. And sometime in there, I have to do my homework." But then, doing homework on the road during racing season is nothing new for Sarah.

Although by anyone's standards, Sarah is playing in the big leagues now, she and Walker realize that there is still a long way to go.

"Sarah is very good, but she's still new at racing in this series. She needs more seat time. In this sport you evolve yourself and the car," says Walker. "You always have to drive with confidence. You are either an idiot or you believe the car will do what you expect it to do. Once you have confidence, then you know how aggressive you can be in a given situation. In a sport where races are often decided by tenths of a second, being cautious is the difference between being first and last. The secret is to understand how to push yourself and the car—just to the edge but not beyond. The minute you start to question yourself, you will begin losing.

"In racing, winning is really the only thing that matters. If a female wins, well, that's something. But in a big money sport like this, the novelty alone isn't worth much. That girl must win if she's going to survive. Right now I think Sarah is the only girl in the world that can drive a car of this caliber. She's just amazing. She's elevated herself to this level, but, of course, she won't take my word for it."

"Being a race car driver has been my goal, my fantasy my whole life," says Sarah. When I passed the rookie test in Las Vegas, I realized that I could realistically compete in big races like the Indy 500. When Tony George said he was looking for young talent who could start gaining exposure in a major race, I knew I had the chance."

"Sarah has made the transition from running a sprint to running a marathon," says Walker. "She still gets nervous before a race, but once the flag is waved, she calms right down. She's such a fast learner. She's been around only one season, but already she sounds like she's been here for 50 years. She's like a sponge. She soaks up whatever you tell her.

"She's very committed because she's doing what she wants to do. I think she's within sight of victory, but there are still a lot of tests ahead of her. It's one thing to be the up and comer, but now that she's passed that stage in her career, the expectations will be a lot different. She has to learn that she won't always win, that sometimes she won't even make the race. We'll both have to be patient. This is not a sport that you learn to do overnight."

"This has been an awesome year," says Sarah. I can't imagine that there will be another one like it for a long time. So much has happened that honestly, it would be hard to pick a single highlight," she says. "Certainly running for the first time in the Indy 500 was one. Standing on the podium with Derrick in Kentucky was a tremendous thrill. The most important thing, though, was just the experience of being a part of this organization. We've really come together this year and begun to gel as a team. As Derrick says, 'in racing winning is really the only thing that matters' and that's what he and I are here to do."

2

Never Be Afraid to Try Something New

A Profile of Gretchen Hammarberg—Wakeboarder

From the sunny coast of California to the lakes of upstate New York and just about everywhere in between, wakeboarding may be the fastest growing water sport in America. A hybrid of surfing, snowboarding, and waterskiing, this sport involves athletes being dragged 55 to 80 feet behind boats traveling 18-25 miles per hour, launching themselves 20 or more feet in the air and doing a series of twists, turns and jumps that scarcely seem possible. One common theme prevails: a need for big air, extreme tricks and a healthy dose of adrenaline.

Wakeboarding brings with it the next generation of athletes and their fans, who, not surprisingly, considering the risky nature of the sport, are mostly in their late teens and early twenties. Like its sister sports, in-line skating and snowboarding, the crowd it draws also tends to be cool and laid back.

Surfer Tony Finn is credited with founding the sport of wakeboarding in San Diego in 1985. After watching his surfer buddies being towed on regular surfboards behind a ski boat or truck on shore, Finn wondered what would happen if a board were designed specifically for this purpose. He began to experiment and the result was a 'skurfer,' a cross between a slalom water ski and a surfboard. Still mostly resembling the surfboard, it was shorter and narrower and those who tried it out compared it to the feel of a snowboard or skateboard.

While the way the board handled when being towed was a vast improvement over the conventional surfboard, it lacked one fundamental component – something to hold the skurfer's feet to the board when the towing vehicle picked up speed. Two of Finn's windsurfer friends, Mike and Mark Pascoe provided the solution to Finn's problem. They gave him a pair of foot straps and inserts to attach to the skurfer. Skiboarding, a primitive form of wakeboarding, was born.

For the next few years, Finn promoted and popularized this more exciting variation of waterskiing. The sport quickly gained popularity among advanced skiers and surfers. In June 1987 at Soda Lakes in Lakewood, Colorado, skurfing made its national debut as an expression session at a slalom and kneeboard tournament.

In 1990, the Skurfer Championships were televised on ESPN.

Skurfing as a sport, however, was still limited to only the very strongest skiers, since, due to the buoyant boards, it required a deep water start. After watching the championships, Herb O'Brien, owner of H.O. Water Sports, came up with the solution to this problem. Working with some of Hawaii's best surfboard shapers, O'Brien developed the Hyperlite, a neutral buoyancy and compression-molded wakeboard. This board made it possible for riders to easily submerge the board while also allowing the board to stay on top of the water once the rider got up. The twin-tip board that permitted a rider to ride with either foot forward, similar to the way snowboards are designed, was a further O'Brien improvement.

Sensing the growing popularity of the sport, Jimmy Redmond founded the World Wakeboarding Association, now *the worldwide governing body for the sport. Rules, formats and point systems were developed, a professional wakeboarding tour was organized and it soon began to receive the publicity and support necessary for the sport to grow. And grow it has. The World Wakeboarding Championship for pros is now televised regularly on ESPN and thousands of grassroots tournaments, open to wakeboarders of all skill levels, are held around the nation.*

* * *

The summer sun is high in the sky and record temperatures have resulted in a heat wave, sweltering the American Northwest. Like many of the citizens of Coeur d'Alene, Idaho on this hot, muggy day, Gretchen Hammarberg is out on the waters of Lake Hayden. In fact, much of the lake's surface is dotted with pontoons and speedboats, filled with people trying to beat the heat. Most are relaxing over an early morning coffee or dangling a fishing line hopefully over the side of a fishing boat.

But not Gretchen. For the past five hours—long before most of her fellow boaters even thought about getting up—she's been out on the water doing some serious work. Just moments ago, to the absolute amazement of boaters nearby, she curved through the water, nailed the wake at 21 miles an hour, launched herself seventeen feet in the air, executed a layout back flip over the wake, pulled the rope hard with her right hand, passed it to her left behind her back, spun 180 degrees away from the boat and landed deftly back on her feet.

"Tantrum to blind. I can't believe you just landed that," yells her best friend, Kelly, from the driver's seat of the boat.

As the boat pulls along side, Gretchen dips her hair in the water. It's the end of a long day of practice, but it's been a good one. She now feels confident about adding yet another difficult maneuver to her repertoire. And, furthermore, she knows she's one of the few women, if not the only woman, able to do it. It's no surprise she's considered one of the premier wakeboarders in the Northwest Sessions semi-pro division.

A series of the amateur wakeboarding tour, the Northwest Sessions, held in Idaho, Montana and Washington, are contests ranging in skill level from beginner to semi-pro. "They were designed in response to the big wakeboarding scene in this part of the country," says Gretchen. Although she is arguably plenty good enough to consider a pro career, she has, up to this point, preferred these meets to the pro tour. "The same people usually come to these meets, so it's like a vacation weekend where you get to wakeboard and also party with all your friends," she says. "The Northwest Sessions are also a ton of fun because I'm one of the few girls who even rides in the contests. I tend to get a bit of attention."

It was this merited attention by some of the top semi-pro judges that qualified her for the nationals of the World Wakeboarding Championships held in Orlando in 2000. Gretchen describes this event as one of her most memorable wakeboarding experiences to date. "I just decided to pick up and take time off school and was fortunate enough to be able to live with Andrea Gaytan for three months," she says. "Andrea paved the road for female wakeboarders and, at that time, was the most talented female professional wakeboarder in the world.

"Andrea was injured at that point and wouldn't go near the boat but she was very generous and let me use it," says Gretchen. "It was cool. I had an amazing adventure, made a great friend and created some good connections in the world of wakeboarding. I ended up winning one of Andrea's signed boards and met all of the people I had seen in the magazines and on the videos."

On the first day at the Orlando competition, Gretchen placed first in the preliminaries, granting her a berth in the finals. "The judges were taking their sweet time figuring the scores," she says, "but I didn't even think about it because I didn't think it was my best run. It was pretty rad when I heard my name announced as first, especially since my main sponsor from Krown Wakeboards and a lot of my good wakeboarding buddies were sitting right next to me. I was pretty stoked." She went on to take third overall in the nation at the semi-pro level, the highest amateur division.

"The whole thing was a lot of fun," she says, "but I realized I didn't want to devote my entire life to wakeboarding at that time. I was still trying to evaluate where my thoughts on wakeboarding stood. I was at sort of a crossroads in my life where I needed to decide whether to either focus entirely on wakeboarding at a competitive level or continue to do it passionately as I had been, but not so seriously."

While it was tempting to try to move up, Gretchen chose, instead, to go back to her studies at the University of Colorado, Boulder. Just as Sarah Fisher's degree in mechanical engineering will complement her sport—auto racing—so will Gretchen's. This year she'll receive her BS in psychology. "I studied kineseology for the first couple of years," she says, "then switched my major to psychology in hopes of one day combining the knowledge of both fields into counseling athletes in sports psychology."

Unlike Sarah Fisher, who has chosen to schedule college around racing, Gretchen has done just the opposite, scheduling wakeboarding around school. But with the prospect of graduation in the near future, she has now made the decision to postpone the start of her career in psychology to spend more time competing.

This decision will not, however, be without its challenges, the first being financial. "Although my sponsor, Krown, is really great, they're not a huge company, so they don't have a lot of money to dish out for all the competitions," says Gretchen. "So some of the entry fees even in the semi-pro circuit have had to come from my family or from my part-time job. And those fees aren't cheap."

She's also torn between moving up to the pro circuit or staying with Northwest Sessions. "The scene we have in Idaho really inspires me because it's a lot of fun and everyone helps me out," she says. "I almost feel like the other competitors are part of my family. Also, technically, I'm still undiscovered, so I don't want to make a bad name for myself before I make up my mind about exactly where I want to go with the sport."

Compared to most avid wakeboarders, Gretchen's season and practice time has been extremely limited. Because she has grown up in Idaho and attended college in Colorado, unlike the majority of professional wakeboarders who live primarily in Florida or California, she has only been able to get out on the water a few months a year. Most of the riders on the pro tour train in the water virtually all year around. To compensate, she says she has stayed involved athletically in other sports, cross training in the mountains. During a typical week, she jogs three or four miles to class five days a week, bikes and hikes. "Staying in shape is something I've done forever," she says, "so that's not really training as much as doing what I would do anyway. I also snowboard. That helps me for style and some of the tricks."

Gretchen's snowboarding expertise may be even more of a help to her in the future. Although the competitive style of wakeboarding still reflects its West Coast beginnings, according to Gretchen, in many ways it is starting to look a lot more like snowboarding. Some courses now include sliders and ramps made out of PVC pipes or a comparable material, similar to those found in snowboard and in-line skate parks. These additions allow riders to make rail slides or higher jumps for really big tricks.

Like Lynn Hill, Gretchen was a competitive gymnast so she understood the mechanics of wakeboarding long before she strapped on bindings for the first time. "Gymnastics plays a lot into why I can pick up on certain flips fairly easily," she says. "It is also why my spins and grabs are not the most exciting thing to watch. Spinning is generally considered the most difficult part of wakeboarding because there are so many variations depending on how much spin is involved, which direction the person is spinning in relation to the boat and in what direction the wakeboarder approaches the wake. The most important thing is that I'm a quick learner. You should never be afraid to try something new."

As with most athletes, Gretchen finds that psychology plays a big part in how she performs on any given day. "I usually have the courage to try most wakeboarding tricks if I've never been hurt doing them or haven't had enough time to think about all the possible outcomes," she says. "But like most things in sports, it's all mental. If I catch myself on a head case day, I might choose not to try a certain trick because I can easily defeat myself more than anyone else can."

Yet she finds that others can also snap her out of it. "Who I'm riding with and how the day is going is often as important as the intensity of the trick and how easily I'll try it," she says.

"Who I ride with has a lot to do with my drive. Other people can be very motivating to me if I'm not able to motivate myself that day."

The ability to conquer fear is what traditionally distinguishes elite athletes from the average participant, especially in extreme sports where other factors such as speed or risky moves are involved. "As long as I understand the mechanics of the trick, I usually don't have a lot of fear of the water," says Gretchen. "I try not to think about the danger most of the time. Fear isn't something that naturally comes into my head. But fear can creep into all of us. If I see someone get injured or I get hurt or even if someone tells a story about someone getting hurt doing a trick that I want to try, it definitely makes me think about what could happen. Ultimately, I try to stay away from negative thoughts. If you think negatively too long, you can cause a negative outcome."

Even so, with tricks like the Air Raley, where the rider flies like Superman behind the boat or the Mobius, where the rider does a flip over the wake with a handle pass, the water can pose great risk to the rider. "I remember when I was learning to do a 180," says Gretchen. "It was raining and cold outside and I had been trying for 30 minutes to do it. On my last declared try, I fell and my board came off. When I came up out of the water the board hit me squarely in the head. By the time the boat came around to pick me up, I had pretty well decided to quit for the day. Kelly, my driver looked down at me and said, 'Yeah, I think you're through.' As it turned out the board had made this big cut in my head and I was bleeding quite profusely."

Luckily, the head injury Gretchen incurred in that practice session is the only injury she's received other than the normal bumps and bruises that go along with any competitive sport.

Like many of her sister athletes, Gretchen strongly believes that enjoyment of the sport is necessary for success. "A rider has to be having fun," she says. "Two of the most important things, especially in contests, are that you are having fun and you are relaxed. If you don't have those two things working for you, the slightest mistake or mental issue can completely throw your whole competition off." She adds, "I also have to chew gum. Chewing gum helps me relax and take things less seriously."

Gretchen doesn't technically have a coach. "I learn from the crew I ride with," she says. "They do it more as a passion than a competition, although I think they are extremely talented. We all coach each other when we go ride. It's really cool, because the advice we give each other is free and we all have a great time."

She finds training with friends helps with the burnout that a lot of competitive athletes face as a result of extensively training year in and year out. "Too often talented athletes focus so much on constant improvement that they lose sight of the truly important issues involved in the sport," she says. "They drive themselves until they quit, or worse, end up hating the sport altogether. My friends, and everyone I have had the opportunity to ride with, inspire me and keep me loving the sport."

Having so much fun training does have a downside, she admits. "Sometimes because I'm having such a great time, I play around too much. We are definitely always learning new tricks and working on consistency with the ones I know, but as far as practicing a competition pass, which is ultimately important, well, we sometimes don't practice it as often as we should."

Even after seven years of serious wakeboarding, five years of competition, and an impressive list of accomplishments, Gretchen clearly recalls an early setback.

"My first-ever pro stop was in Hartford, Connecticut," she recalls. "It was probably the most embarrassing and disappointing moment I've ever had in this sport. I had traveled all the way from Idaho to Connecticut to perform in front of a large crowd that included my father, stepmother, an uncle and a few of my cousins. Since I didn't have a ranking on the tour, I had to ride first in the prelims to be able to ride in the semis and then possibly the finals. A wakeboarding course is set up with a buoy at each end, one to indicate the start and the other to signify the end of the first pass where the boat and rider must turn to complete the second pass. On each pass, a rider usually executes five to seven tricks with a 'double up,' at the end of the pass, where the boat makes a wide turn around the buoy so the rider can launch off both wakes to perform a really big trick. The rider is allowed one continuation after a fall. If the rider falls a second time, her run is over and the judges give a score based on the tricks that were completed.

"When I rode, I fell on like my third trick," she says. "Then I had to wait for the boat to turn around before there was enough speed to start my next pass. While the boat was turning around, I was on the inside of the turn. It made a sharper turn than I expected and I sunk to my neck. Because I was still on the course, that was considered my second fall. Needless to say, I didn't make it past the prelims. Thirty seconds and a bunch of money later, my first contest was over."

After her disappointing last place finish in her first year of competition in Hartford, she went on to grab tenth place in

Denver and a seventh place finish in Abbotsford, Vancouver on the pro-level. Opting for the semi-pro level for the next four years, she competed in the Northwest Sessions stops in Sandpoint, Idaho; Kalispell, Montana; Bellevue and Olympia Washington, where she qualified for the 2000 nationals in Orlando, taking first place in each competition each year. In Orlando, she took first place in the preliminaries and finished third overall in the nation as a semi-pro.

In addition to that, she competed in INT Tour Stop (similar to the pro tour) in Boulder while she was in school, taking second in the men's amateur division. In 1998, she also competed for the Overton Boat Company in a Fox Sports TV water sport contest in San Diego, which was sponsored by Slash of Guns 'N Roses plus two other events in St. Paul. These were team-based competitions, combining trick skiing, ski jumping, slaloming and wakeboarding. Her team placed second in the first two competitions and fourth in the last competition, collecting more than $1,500.

Even though she describes her approach to training as relaxed, Gretchen is extremely disciplined when it comes to preparing herself mentally for the season. As early as January, when three feet of snow still covers the streets of Boulder, she begins visualizing the mechanics of her tricks, practicing them on a snowboard. When spring approaches, she concentrates more on upper body lifting so she has the arm strength to get ready for riding.

Her season begins virtually the day she finishes classes. "I try to ride as many times in May as possible, but the weather in Colorado in May can be pretty unpredictable," she says. "Also, equipment is not always available—namely my boat." Starting her season in earnest in June, she usually rides about five to seven sessions a week. She maintains this schedule through August until she returns to school.

Training nine months for a three-month season may seem over zealous to the average person, but Gretchen doesn't think so. "I compete because I feel it is part of the sport," she says. "Although a lot of people in the wakeboarding industry have a negative attitude about contests, I think competition shows a skill that some people may not have. It's one of the ultimate mental exercises. On any given day, the mind can get in the way of all your preparation. That adds an awesome factor to the sport. Competition requires the mental preparedness and confidence to perform in a high stress situation.

"I guess if I could wish for one thing, it would be to have the ability to control my emotions better. I'm envious of people who always seem to be in the right frame of mind to compete. Oddly enough, I find that I sometimes perform much better if I'm the dark horse. That may not always be the best approach. But sometimes it works for me."

Still, she admits to a highly competitive streak. "I get my motivation from the competitive part of my personality," she says. "I love sports in general and I especially love the feeling you get when you exercise—the feeling you get when you know you've accomplished something. Once you have a passion for something, the motivation comes with it. Competition feeds this for me. That's why I'm a lot more bummed out than many people when I do poorly in a contest. I have strong emotions and a lot of drive."

"There's also a lot more at stake if you compete," she says. "Everyone in the industry pushes the level of riding because if you want to stay in the game and want to keep your sponsors, you have to stay above the others. It's a constant battle. But you can never win if you psych yourself out. If your drive doesn't come from within to begin with, whatever the other people do doesn't matter."

As women's wakeboarding becomes increasingly more popular, Gretchen has seen the competition get fiercer. "From my past experience to now," she says, "I've noticed an increase in the number of girls of all levels out there riding, including some bad ass little rippers who pop out of nowhere. The age range of women's wakeboarding as well as men's is getting younger so I can foresee the competition getting more intense and the skill level becoming increasingly greater."

At the moment, however, compared to men, there still aren't a lot of women competing. "I find that I'm generally more competitive with women than men," she says. "Other good women riders motivate me more because I know I can do what they do and I want to be able to prove it. I'm anxious for more women to get into competition. Women still have a nice opportunity to be the first to do a lot of the tricks that men already do. Also, I believe that the ultimate trick for women is still up in the air because there is quite a large gap between women's and men's riding abilities. Learning the new trick is the ultimate accomplishment," she says.

"Wakeboarding has the potential to increase both money and opportunity for women," says Gretchen. "However, at present there are still a lot of politics involved in wakeboarding as there are in most sports. Women still don't make nearly as much in prize money, although to be honest, men usually have five times more competitors than the women.

"The men are also throwing bigger tricks at the moment," she says, "although women are stepping up to the challenge.

Still, when women sign a contract, their monthly salary is still lower than a male with comparable reputation.

"For the most part," says Gretchen, "I feel like I'm treated pretty well in this sport. When you are one of the only girls who wakeboards and you are well respected by the men, you tend to get even more attention than a man who is awesome but is average in a field of ten other guys."

3

The Wind is Your Friend, The Wind Will Make You Strong

A Profile of Heather Hedrick—Triathlete

Although men and women have been competing in swimming and running events for thousands of years and have been cycling for at least 100 years, the three were not combined into a single event until 1974. That's not to say there weren't earlier events called triathlons. The 1904 Olympic Games, for example, included a triathlon consisting of a long jump, shot put and 100-yard dash.

The closest thing to the modern triathlon was held in 1921 in Marseilles, France, the Petit Perillon swim club's Course Des Trois Sports, consisting of a 7K bicycle race, a 5K run and a 200 meter out and back swim.

The San Diego Track Club is credited with organizing the first official US triathlon in 1974. The six-mile run, five-mile bike race and 500-yard swim, was held not so much to make history as to celebrate club member Dave Pain's 50th birthday.

But the idea caught on. And, as in many sports, the next group to try it decided to make it harder. In 1978, fifteen com-

petitors participated in the first Ironman Triathlon, a full 26.2 mile marathon, 112 mile bike race and 2.4 mile swim. While the San Diego event had taken just under an hour, the Ironman took nearly a half day—11 hours, 46 minutes, 58 seconds.

In 1982, the sport was officially organized, the governing body the United States Triathlon Association (USTA). That same year the USTA sanctioned the Torrey Pines Triathlon and paid out its first prize money. In 1983, the organization name was changed to Triathlon Federation/USA.

Unlike many sports that were at first dominated by men, from the beginning, the triathlon has been a co-ed event. More than 10 women competed in the San Diego Track Club event and the sole female Ironman competitor, Julie Moss, received considerable media coverage as she crawled across the finish line to take second place.

Today, the sport is highly organized with all sorts of qualifying events required for entry into the more prestigious events like the Ironman. Since 1995, the triathlon has been an official event of the Pan American Games and became a medal sport for the 2000 Olympic Games.

* * *

It's a cold, blustery day in early spring. While most of her fellow Hoosiers are cuddling a blanket up around their chins and rolling over for another hour or so of sleep, Heather Hedrick sits on the bumper of her car, laces up her shoes and fastens her helmet. As the sun appears over the horizon and begins to melt the frost on the corn and soybean fields, she pulls her bike off the rack and onto a lonely country road. With a chilly west wind blowing directly in her face, she sets off on a 60-mile ride. She knows it will be cold and it won't be much fun. If it's a typical day, she'll probably be chased by a couple of barnyard dogs and blown sideways by a pickup truck or two, barreling past her at 60 miles an hour, covering her with gravel dust. But this ride and countless others like it are what Heather knows she must do if she is to reach her goal – to be one of the top triathletes in the world.

She's off to a good start. Within the last three years, among other things she's placed first among women in five triathlons and three duathlons, placed in the top 4% of women in the Boston Marathon, placed third in the 25-29 year age group among women in the Powerman Alabama Duathlon, placed first among women two years in a row in the Mideast Regional Triathlon and placed third among US female athletes in the World Duathlon Championship in Calais, France. And, she was just awarded All-American status for duathlon in 2000 by USA Triathlon.

By anyone's standards she's an accomplished athlete. Although some might say an unlikely athlete, given her background. Unlike many of the nation's best and brightest who started training as soon as they were out of diapers, she wasn't an athlete at all until she was in her early 20s.

"The most athletic thing I did in high school was cheerleading," she admits.

Going off to the University of Illinois for a degree in dietetics changed all that. For the first time in her life, Heather began to think seriously about a healthier lifestyle. She became a vegetarian. She cut out red meat, then fish (which she didn't like much, anyway), then chicken. Soon she gave up the eggs, cheese and skim milk that had become a staple in her diet. A stint in the animal lab while working on her master's thesis later firmed up her resolve.

"The move away from eating animals and animal products was part health, part political statement," she says. "I think that we can come up with better ways to feed the world's people."

In graduate school, working toward a degree in exercise physiology, Heather bought her first "real" bike and got serious about exercise.

"Well, kind of serious," she says. "The first long distance bike ride I did was the RAGBRAI (Register's Annual Great Bike Ride Across Iowa) which is essentially a big excuse to party all the way across the state."

Finding, to her surprise, that she enjoyed the ride as much as the partying, once back at U of I, she began training in earnest.

"A couple of guys I knew got me interested in running and before I knew it, I was entering my first race, the Champaign Urbana Mayor's Duathlon. I surprised myself by doing really well."

Well indeed. In the first duathlon she'd ever entered she beat every other female competitor.

After that victory, the guys she'd been training with suggested that she begin to take the sport seriously.

"So off we'd go out onto those country roads in central Illinois," says Heather. "They are so, so flat and so, so windy. Out there on those really cold days I'd be freezing and muttering. 'Heather, the wind is your friend. The wind will make you strong,' they'd keep saying. It made me crazy to hear that!"

After receiving her master's degree, she landed a job as the assistant director of the Center for Educational Services at National Institute for Fitness and Sport (NIFS) and moved to Indianapolis. In short order she was entering and winning local races one after another and placing near the top in regional and national events.

With the victories, however, came the injuries. Her 3:14 finish in the Chicago Marathon in 1997 qualified her for the Boston Marathon but a serious stress fracture of the femur kept her out of that race and all other competition for four months. Although she came right back to win the Terre Haute (Indiana) Triathlon in 1998, after completing the Boston Marathon in 3:26, another stress fracture – this time of the tibia – took her out of racing for the summer of 1999. In the fall, she was back in competition, again taking first place among females in the Mideast Regional Championship Triathlon in Indianapolis in September and Tyler's Duathlon in Cincinnati in October. But she couldn't get the injuries off her mind.

Her performance at the Blackwater Eagleman Triathlon in Maryland in early June 2000, proved to be a big disappointment. "That race was a qualifier for the Hawaii Ironman and lots of great triathletes were there. I came in 12th in my age group—the lowest I had ever placed in a triathlon. On the drive home I was really upset with how I compared to the other women in my age group. I decided then and there that I had two choices. I could continue to work on my own, enjoy triathlons and not worry about how I placed or get serious about competing, expect more of myself, hire a coach and try my hardest to do the best I could.

"Not everyone has the same philosophy about what it takes to be a serious competitor," says Heather. "I had worked with a coach for a month or so in 1998, but his philosophy was that you needed to keep pushing yourself if you wanted to get better. That meant working out as much as you possibly could, always trying to go farther and faster all the time. I'm

*Heather Hedrick is now one of the top female triathletes
and duathletes in the nation..*

not saying that doesn't work for some people, but in my case, I think it really contributed to my injuries. By always pushing myself to the limit, I never gave my body a chance to recover."

Back in Indianapolis, she called Mike Smith.

"Mike's training philosophy is much more in sync with mine. We both believe that it is important to make every workout meaningful, to have a reason for what we do. Otherwise you're just putting in 'junk miles' that can often cause you more harm than good. We agree that each workout should be done to achieve a specific outcome so that you always have a goal and feel like you have accomplished something when you're finished. You should always be doing enough to improve, but not so much that you wear yourself out just for the sake of it.

"We're also in agreement about injuries. If you get injured, you should rest, not try to push through it and live with the pain. Your body will tell you when something isn't right. You have to listen to what your body says. So far, this philosophy has worked well for me. This is the first year I've gone without an injury."

Heather puts in an impressive weekly workout schedule designed and overseen by Smith. Because of the seasonal nature of her sport and the unpredictability of Midwestern winters, Heather's training regimen is divided into two components. "In season," while she's competing, she does at least some training six days a week, alternating running and biking with swimming. Typically, this means a six mile run and a 30 mile bike ride on Sunday, a 3,500 meter swim on Monday, 50 minutes of spinning, a 25 mile bike ride and a four mile run on Tuesday, another 3,500 meter swim and an eight mile run on Wednesday, an hour to an hour and a half of spinning on Thursday, a rest day on Friday and then a 20 mile bike ride and a four mile run on Saturday. In all, each week she swims 7,000 meters, bikes 120 miles and runs 22 miles. In the off season, she trims back to a five day a week workout schedule. In her spare time, she also manages to work in some weight training and yoga.

Obviously all this training takes a lot of time, especially for someone who has a demanding full time job. Her responsibilities at NIFS include holding seminars on nutrition, fitness and wellness for the community, corporations and national conferences, overseeing training programs for events like the annual Indianapolis Life 500 Festival Mini Marathon, managing the Institute's internship program, editing a newsletter, contributing to numerous fitness-related publications and serving as coordinator of certification for the American College of Sports Medicine.

Fortunately, her job at NIFS offers a good deal of flexibility. In addition, some of her responsibilities, like leading spinning classes, mesh well with her training schedule. It doesn't hurt that her office is located in one of the premiere fitness complexes in the nation. Within a few minutes, she can be out of her business clothes and on the track, on a stationery bike or in the pool. Plus, she has the constant encouragement and support of the fellow athletes she works with every day.

"Having supportive people around you is key," says Heather, who also gives a lot of the credit for her success to her family. "My grandparents, parents and sister always come to watch my races and cheer me on," she says. "Their love and support have meant everything to me."

In addition to strict adherence to a training schedule, as

Heather competes in increasingly bigger and more distant events, she has found that she must pay equal attention to nutrition. Being a registered dietician has been a big help to her in this area.

"If your nutrition is wrong, then your whole race will be wrong," she says. "Because of the endurance aspect of this sport, training and nutrition are equally important. You may be trained to the max, but if your diet is not also disciplined, you'll never be able to achieve your potential. When in training for an extreme sport, you can't just think about calories. You have to be aware of type of calories and the amount of calories that that you take in. Also, what nutrition you require and when you require it is a very individual thing. Two people can be about the same size and weight and train the same amount of time, but if their body chemistry is different, their nutritional needs will be different, too. Obviously, there is a big difference between males and females in body structure, musculature, hormonal balance and so on, but beyond that, there are differences in body composition and genetics, too. You have to take all of that into consideration when deciding what you're going to eat."

Not surprisingly, Heather feels that in addition to a good coach, most serious athletes should get professional help in finding the diet that works for them.

Does she recommend her vegetarian diet for others?

"Not necessarily," she says. "I was a vegetarian long before I became a serious athlete, so my body was already used to it. Others may achieve the same or better results another way.

In addition to knowing what to eat, Heather is also a firm believer in knowing when to eat.

"Again, this is a very individual thing," she says. "It's

Cycling is the strongest of Heather Hedrick's sports.

something you just have to figure out by trial and error. I've found that I do best if I eat four hours before a race, no matter when it starts. So that means if the race starts at 7:00 a.m., I will get up at 3:00 a.m. have some oatmeal, soy milk, a banana and some orange juice and then go back to sleep.

"This drives my racing roommates nuts," she adds, "especially when I then get up two hours later for a cup of coffee and head out to the start of the race.

"As for how much I eat, I've found out over the years that for me, at least, it's best to let my body tell me what it wants. When I first started to compete, I probably wasn't eating enough, so I've tried to work on that."

Although she is skilled at both cycling and running, at first she found combining them into one event a challenge.

"Because you tend to focus so much on what you're doing when you compete, it's really tough to immediately switch gears. I clearly remember the first time I competed in a duathlon. I jumped off the bike and my legs felt completely disconnected from my body. 'Where are my legs?' I said to the guy next to me."

Now she's much more accustomed to what's required.

"After the bike leg of the race, I stop my bike at the entrance of the transition area and run carefully to my spot, place my bike on the rack, rip off my helmet and bike shoes and toss on running shoes with lace locks (an easy way to secure shoes) and my racing belt with my race number attached. This is the last part of the triathlon," she adds, "so I know I'm in the home stretch."

Still, even now it takes her a while to get her legs back. "Even now they tend to feel a little shaky at first, but then I move into my groove and try to run as fast as possible after biking as hard as I can," says Heather. "I try to take a little fluid every other mile, but it's much harder for me to drink while running than while biking. Depending on the length of the run, I may bring along several gels to provide energy. If it's a short race, sports drinks along the way will do.

"After the bike leg of the race, I usually have several more people to catch, so I start to search for them and run as fast as I can to pass them. The speed of my run will depend on the length of the race. For short distances, it's an all-out sprint. In longer races, I go slightly slower than a sprint pace, but something I can maintain. At this point, I start counting down the miles, the steps, the trees – whatever will help me keep my mind off the total distance remaining. I try to break the run into small goals to keep myself going strong."

Adding swimming in order to compete in triathlons was probably the biggest step for Heather.

"Swimming is still my weakest sport," she says, although she feels that she has greatly improved over the past three years training under coach Mel Goldstein at the Indiana University Natatorium in downtown Indianapolis.

She was named Female Triathlete of the Year by the Master's Swim Team, but she still isn't where she wants to be. One thing she says helps is to have a friend stand at the end of the swimming leg of the triathlon and count the number of women who come out of the water ahead of her.

"At the Mideast Championships in 2000, I was a full seven minutes behind the first woman," she says.

So far, since she is such a strong cyclist, she's been able to make up that time in the cycling leg of the event. "But I know I can't keep doing that," she says. "In order to be fully competitive in this event, I have to be equally competitive in all three components."

Another big adjustment was the sheer number of competitors in the bigger events.

"I'll never forget my first triathlon," says Heather. "When you train in swimming, you train in a pool where the closest person is in the next lane. All of a sudden I was in this lake with all these people bumping into me and climbing all over me to get ahead. I was sure I was going to drown. It took me awhile before I could just dive into that mass of humanity and fight my way through."

The fact that triathlons involve lakes was another not so

pleasant experience.

"Once after a race, a friend called me in the middle of the Iowa ride to tell me that the Center for Disease Control had called and confirmed that the lake we'd just been competing in was full of Leptosporosis, which is caused by feces and other generally yucky stuff in the water. She was horribly sick, so I went to the hospital to get checked out. Fortunately, I was all right, but I still think about it. You can't imagine what that lake was like. With everyone thrashing around, when we got out of the water, we were so covered with dirt and grime, it was hard to tell the men from the women."

Although she's now had a good deal more experience with triathlons, she still finds that the start of the swim creates the most anxiety.

"Each wave of competitors has the same color swim cap," says Heather. "We all enter the water at the same time, bouncing around trying to stay above water, anxiously waiting for the sound of the gun. Each person has a different idea about where they want to be at the start. I used to start in at the back and let everyone to go ahead while I waited for them to clear out. Now that I have become braver, I start in the front line. The first 200-500 yards are a constant battle with everyone else's arms and legs while I'm trying to keep my goggles on and stay on track. I find that it helps to keep my eye on the boats or buoys or even other competitors. You have to lift your head and look ahead, even though the sun may be blinding you. You have to do your best and trust your judgement. Believe me, there is nothing sweeter than seeing the flags signifying the end of the swim. I can hardly wait to get out of the water, run like mad to our spot in the transition area, rip off my goggles and cap and shimmy that wet suit off my body."

Because swimming is still not her strongest sport she says, "I am so happy to be done with the swim I can hardly wait to get on the bike. This is often when I realize that I'm really far behind the female leader and know I have my work cut out for me. I throw on my bike shoes, helmet and sunglasses and run to the exit of the transition area."

The bicycling leg of the race follows the swim. "While swimming is my weakest area, biking is my strongest. I love the feeling of going really fast and passing competitor after competitor. I usually know how many women are ahead of me and I can count down on the bike how many I've passed. This leg of the triathlon is also the easiest for consuming fluid and food. I make a point of drinking at every mile marker, taking gel or bars at the perfect time event in small portions so as not to upset my digestive system during the bike leg of the event."

Not surprisingly, Heather prefers flat courses, but even on the flattest legs, she must always be well aware of her position in relation to other competitors. "If you're ever caught drafting, they add minutes to your time, so you want to avoid that at all costs," she says.

How does Heather keep track of how well she's doing in comparison to other women? It's not easy since in both duathlon and triathlon competitions there is tremendous variation from race to race. Distances vary from the 500 meter swim, 13 mile bike ride and 5K run of the Sprints to the 2.5 mile swim, 112 mile bike ride and 26.2 mile run of the Ironman. In between are the half-Ironman, short course, long course and Olympic competitions. And, as if variation in distance doesn't make the sport confusing enough, there is also a huge difference in terrain from event to event.

Heather Hedrick's 3:18:07 time in the Boston Marathon placed her among the top 4% of all women in the race.

"All this makes it very hard to compare how you're doing from race to race," says Heather. "The best you can do is to look at how your pace compares to that of the other women who did the same course.

"Also, I'm discovering that usually you don't really know what you're up against until you get there," says Heather. "Before the World Duathlon Championships in France, we all got maps showing where the course would go and describing it as 'fairly flat.' Training as I do on central Indiana roads, I'm used to flat, flat, flat. According to this map it looked like there was just one hill, so I thought to myself, how hard could that be? When we got there, however, we were in for a big surprise. Their idea of 'fairly flat' was very different from mine. There was a three-mile climb, then a series of switch-backs and then it was all up and down. What they said were hills looked like mountains to me."

In addition to unfamiliar terrain, amateur competitors like Heather face a host of other obstacles. Since most hold full or part time jobs, they can only take so much time off, so they don't have the luxury of arriving at the competition days in advance. Thus, they must be ready to compete at peak level even if they're jet lagged, have a back ache from sleeping in a strange bed or a stomach ache from unfamiliar food.

Although there isn't much Heather can do about the travel, she doesn't take any chances with the food.

"To the extent possible, I just take my own," she says. She found this to be a particular necessity for the French competition. "The French are not exactly famous for their vegetarian cuisine," she says

Unlike many athletes she is not particularly superstitious. But, Heather finds she is more relaxed before a meet if she follows a familiar routine. "I always pack the night before, making sure I have everything I need in my transition bag—towel, swim suit, goggles, cap, suntan lotion, wet suit (if the water is cold enough), Vaseline or Body Glide (to prevent chafing), bike shoes, a race number for the bike, helmet, socks, sunglasses, running shoes, a race number for the run and racing belt, water bottles full of Gatorade and water, gels, bars or other nutrition products for before, during and after the race and finally dry clothes for after the race. I eat dinner no later than 7:00 p.m. I drink a lot of fluids and keep a glass of water beside my bed so I can easily get a drink of water in the middle of the night.

"Whenever possible I get a massage from NIFS message therapist John Elder the day before," she adds. "Also Mike has me run two miles and bike five miles and stretch before each race to warm up. That tends to get me focused."

Once at the race site, she is equally meticulous about unpacking. "Every competitor has a designated spot in the transition area to put the bike, shoes, helmet, water bottles and other items you'll need during the race," says Heather. "I set up my spot very carefully to make sure everything is in order. I also use this time to check out the other competitors, their bikes and equipment and, of course, determine who is there and who the competition for the day will be."

Heather finds there are many advantages to multi-sport events like the duathlon and triathlon.

"Once you get used to the transitions you have to make during the competition, I think the thing that really draws me to this sport is the variety. It keeps you from getting bored with one sport or focusing so much on one thing that if you aren't doing as well as you want, that's all you have. Also, as I've found from personal experience, if you are a little weaker in one area, you can often make up for it in another. I also think that multi-sport competition helps prevent injuries since you don't use the same muscles every time you work out."

Although the events themselves are individual in nature, Heather has found that having some friends to train with is a necessity.

"Sure, training at this level is serious stuff," she says, "but that doesn't mean you can't have fun. When people ask me how to get started with a training program, I tell them to get some books and read up on the subject, consult some experts, get a good coach and, perhaps most importantly, find a partner you like to train with.

"I get such a kick out of the guys I ride with," she says. "Out on these country roads, in addition to the crazy drivers, the biggest threat is dogs. When I find one chasing me, if I can't outbike him, I usually give him a blast of water or Gatorade from my water bottle. But not the men. They feel they have to intimidate the dog so they bark back or yell something like, 'Hey, you, dog, come and get me!' Honestly, it's such a guy thing."

Even though Heather has now achieved national and international recognition in her sport, she finds she still enjoys the local races.

"Competing on the same course and with the same people you train with is just a lot of fun," says Heather. "Even though it can get competitive, it's like a day out with your friends."

Men still outnumber women in duathlon and triathlon competitions, but Heather sees that gradually changing.

"Women are becoming increasingly interested in multi-sport events," she says. "I see a lot more club teams forming and now that there are more women competing, women can compare notes with other women and set goals to match what they see others doing. There is also more media coverage of multi-sport events which means that there are now more companies interested in sponsorship. The more sponsorship, obviously, the more events there will be, which, in turn, will mean that more women will become interested. Also, this was a huge year for the triathlon since it was the first year it was in the Olympics.

"Unlike many other sports, this is also an easy one to become involved in," says Heather. "Since it isn't a team sport, you can do it alone or with your family or a group of friends. All you need are shoes, a swimsuit, a bike and some-place to go. You can also start out slow and find out what you can do. Chances are, no matter what your skill level, there will be events in which you can be competitive if you want to. And, this is a sport you can compete in or just enjoy through-out your life."

To illustrate this point Heather describes a recent job she took on as a consultant.

"I was the dietician for the Race Across America cycling event for a team of four men all over 70," she says. "Two of them hadn't even started exercising until they were over 50. My job was to prepare all their food and do things like weigh them before and after a shift, monitor their hydration and measure their urine. It was a real experience and a great inspiration to me. It made me realize that although we tend to think of competition as being for the young, many people over 60 can be very competitive."

Has Heather considered turning pro?

"Sure, I've been tempted," she says. "I'm very competitive and so I always want to move to the next level. Right now, having to balance job and training, I can't focus all my energy on training. I have to just learn to be more time efficient. Now that my sport is gaining popularity and there is more sponsorship interest, it's possible for the really top athletes to make a living at it. So, yeah, I've thought about it. Until recently," she adds, "my only financial sponsor is my grandfa-ther who paid my way to France and my equipment supplier was a women in my spinning class who is a Nike sales rep."

Just recently, she received her first formal sponsorship from the soy protein bar company, Healthy Soylutions who will provide product, race gear and race entry fees.

"On the other hand, there are some things about amateur status that are gratifying, too. Having 'another life' outside competition may help keep me from burning out although I've found with so much on my plate at once, my social life is pretty much limited to the people I train with.

That seems to have its advantages, too.

"I'm never the party pooper," says Heather. "Everyone else goes home at 10:00 p.m., too."

As the spring sun rises higher in the sky, it warms up a bit, but the wind still rattles last fall's cornstalks and pushes against the front of Heather's bike. As she gears up for another day out on the road with the dogs and the pickup trucks and heaven knows what else, she slides her forearms a little lower on the handlebars. Although she's done this routine hundreds of times before and will do it hundreds of times more, somehow she can't help chuckling a little as again and again she finds herself repeating, "The wind is my friend. The wind will make me strong."

4

It's Not About Getting to the Top, It's About How You Get There

A Profile of Lynn Hill—Rock Climber

Although women had been climbing mountains for hundreds, if not thousands of years (see introduction to Kristen Lignell story) the emergence of rock climbing as a sport is relatively new. Almost anyone can climb a rock face to some degree and, as a result, dozens of climbing sub-sports have evolved. Serious rock climbers divide those sub sports into two categories: free climbing and aid climbing. Even within these categories, there are numerous variations, but, in general, free climbing is defined as climbing without the help of equipment or technology, (except what is required for safety). Aid climbing, conversely, is climbing with the help of pitons, bolts and other gear attached to the wall to give the climber a firmer grip. In some cases aid climbers put all the gear in place and then essentially pull themselves up the rock.

By the 1960s, as more and more people became interested in the sport, repeated ascents of popular walls were beginning to take their toll on the rock. In some locations permanent climbing aids were attached to walls and climbers were restricted to using them. Specially designed nuts, and later spring-loaded camming devices allowed climbers to ascend faster without breaking up the rock surface.

While the amount of time a competitor requires to reach the top is one determinant of success, more importantly to competitors is the degree of difficulty. How long it takes to get to the top is generally far less important than how hard it was to get there. Until the 1980s, rock climbing was strictly an outdoor sport. As it gained popularity, however, a few gyms and outfitters began erecting indoor climbing walls. While these indoor climbing walls are often challenging, most are used strictly for practice or for teaching beginners to climb.

Although rock climbing is now enjoyed by thousands of men and women, for years, it was a decidedly male-dominated sport. That is, until Lynn Hill burst onto the rock climbing scene just over twenty years ago.

In 1979, Lynn made the first ascent of Ophir Broke, rated a 5.12/13a and considered, at that time, the hardest climb ever attempted by a woman. Following that historic climb, Lynn continued to dominate the sport for women, winning the World Cup in 1989 and becoming the first woman to climb the 5.14a Masse Critique in Cimai, France. At that time, a 5.10 was still considered the hardest climb in the US. (Currently a 5.15 is considered the toughest climb in the world). During the 1980s, Lynn either placed in or won every competition she entered. In 1992, Lynn again captured the spotlight. She becoming the first person, let alone woman, to complete a free ascent of The Nose on El Capitan at Yosemite National Park, considered by most rock climbers to be the toughest climb in the world. She further astounded the rock climbing world by going back and doing it again in 1993 in less than 24 hours.

Although Lynn retired from competitive climbing in 1992, her free climbing record of The Nose at El Capitan still stands.

*   *   *

Lynn Hill is a legend. Although she is now officially retired from competition, articles and TV specials about the sport invariably mention her. She is still considered the best example of what women can strive to accomplish in this sport.

It was perhaps inevitable that this be so.

By age 14, Lynn was an accomplished gymnast, but age 14 is often the end, not the beginning of a gymnastics career and, anyway, she says she didn't have much interest in pursuing it to a higher level such as the Olympics. "I was also tired of the conformity and rigidity of repeating the same routines all the time," says Lynn. "I enjoyed the new tricks, but I was tired of the monotony of this form of training." Although very petite, she was strong for a kid her age. But most girls in 1975 weren't yet encouraged to play many of the sports that commonly welcome them today.

What did interest her, though, was the sport her brother and her sister's boyfriend were into: rock climbing.

"I started by climbing trees, light poles, anything I could find," says Lynn. "From the first moment I knew it would be perfect for me. When I discovered climbing, I fell in love with the outdoors, the freedom of movement and the sense of discovery it brought me. You have to remember that this was before anything was written about the sport. There weren't any climbing walls at the local outfitter or stories about climbers on television. The only role models I had were my friends and relatives."

Although there were no manuals or Web sites to educate her on even the basics of the sport, she found that she could easily visualize what climbing would be like. "I talked those guys into taking me with them," she says, "and I immediately fell in love with it."

She found to her delight that she already knew the basics. "The principles were the same as gymnastics," she says. "The difference was in how the moves were performed. Gymnastics is very regimented. You have to do very specific moves and repeat the same movements time and time again. Once up on the rock, I found that climbing let me use my gymnastic skills, but in a way that offered much more freedom and spontaneity."

Although women had not yet achieved the support and notoriety they would in decades to come, Lynn feels that the 1970s was still a good time to begin to pursue her sport seriously. "When I was growing up, Donna de Varona and Billie Jean King had become positive role models," says Lynn. "Title IX (of the Education Amendments Act passed by Congress in 1972) had begun to mandate that women's sports be given at least some measure of equality with men's in the nation's schools. And California, where I was, was one of the first states to take that legislation seriously. We even had a girl's gymnastics program in my high school—which, ironically has now been eliminated due to budget cuts. A lot of women were striving for equality then. There were protests and a lot of questioning of authority. It was a good time to be trying something new. Because I was so small and even though I was still young, I knew that I would never be able to do the things the way the guys did them. I had to rely on my own intuition to figure out the best way for me. But I was also not limited by what other people thought a little girl was capable of. I could accomplish the same things, only in a different way. From a young age, I learned to look for solutions that were appropriate for my own personal dimensions. That has always been the key to my success in climbing."

Although she's often been labeled an "extreme" athlete, Lynn says she doesn't like that term. "Extreme to me means doing something that is dangerous and risky. And that was never my motivation as a climber. The reason I climb is more about learning about myself as well as the sense of partnership with my climbing partners within the natural environment. It has nothing to do with how dangerous it is. I consider what I have done and still do as being more like one of the martial arts. It involves listening to your inner voice. Using your intuition. Focusing on the whole."

Doing things in a dangerous and risky way is, in fact, the very opposite of what Lynn does or advocates. "Climbing is not something most people can just go out one afternoon and do," she says. "It requires a lot of training and a serious focus on mastering your skills. It is not about going out there and conquering something—proving that you are somehow stronger than other people or the rock you're about to climb. It is much more about interacting with your environment."

It's also not a sport like wakeboarding that relies on fancy tricks or spectacular moves. Or a sport like auto racing or the Arctic Man competition that rely on machines and speed. "Climbing is a sport that requires patience and concentration," says Lynn. "When you climb you focus on the essentials. You have to know what your body is doing at all times. It is a very personal thing."

Movies like *Cliffhanger* give the impression that the sport is mostly about macho and muscle bound guys barely surviving one dangerous situation after another. Lynn considers that portrayal of the sport just another Hollywood fantasy.

"You will never get anywhere in climbing until you can achieve a harmonious relationship with the rock," she says. "To someone who's never done it before, it may look dangerous, but if you know what you're doing, you never try to do risky things. Even if you are just out climbing for the afternoon, you'll soon find that this is basically a sport that requires a certain level of endurance. Although bouldering may be the exception, since it requires primarily power. Once you get started up the rock face, your goal is to get to the top. As you continue to challenge yourself, you find that because what you do is increasingly difficult, your goal always is to find the path of least resistance. Sometimes the hardest part of the climb is at the very end, so you want to conserve energy as much as you can. Every climb is an opportunity to grow as a person and learn how to use your body more efficiently.

"I guess this whole 'extreme' movement is somehow an attempt to try to recreate the 1960s," says Lynn. "Maybe some people think that there's something to be gained by 'defying' nature the way the young people in the 1960s defied authority. I'm not sure. I just know that that's not the way I do things."

When Lynn started climbing, the sport was a male-dominated one as, in many ways, it still is. But that didn't, and doesn't, stop her. "I always just took the fact that I was a female doing this sport for granted. When I was growing up, a lot of my friends called me a tomboy because I was always wanting to do the things the boys did. I said, OK, call me a tomboy. Even then, I was able to follow my dreams. I was never afraid to be an individual."

"I think that climbing The Nose at El Capitan did a lot to change some stereotypes in general," says Lynn. "When I did that climb it was literally and figuratively in front of the guys' noses. It is without question the most famous big wall climb in the world. Before I did it, it had never been free climbed. I think, among other things, one of the reasons I was able to climb it was because I was the first person with the right collection of skills and a desire to find the right way to do it. I looked for the possibilities. Again, that goes back to my theory about adaptation. I knew I could adapt my personal ability to that climb."

When contemplating a particularly difficult and challenging climb like El Capitan, many climbers would opt for what is known in the sport as an aid climb. What that means is that the climber attaches ropes to the rock face and essentially pulls him or herself up. What Lynn did—free climbing —involves a rope, but it is only used as a safety line, to break her fall, should she slip.

"My goal was to climb the entire route from top to bottom all free without using my safety equipment for aid in ascending the rock face. I really wanted to explore the natural features of the rock," says Lynn. "To free climb it was to make a statement about what is possible with the right attitude and motivation."

Lynn and a friend climbed The Nose in 1993 in four days. "Then the following year, I did it again in 23 hours," she says. "This is a feat that has not been repeated since. Only one guy has free climbed the entire route, taking 261 days over a three-year period to make his free ascent in 12 days."

She found that the climb required a good deal of both mental and physical skill. "It was like the marathon of climbing," she says. "The best way I can describe it is that it was like all that would be required to do a 100-foot climb applied to a 3,000-foot climb." According to Lynn, the climb is complicated by the fact that the easiest parts of the ascent are at the bottom, with the very hardest at the top. "I knew that I would have to be very efficient and not waste energy," she says. "I had to be completely focused and have faith in my ability."

There are certainly many ways to assess the success of a climb. By most people's standards, the fact that Lynn made it to the top at all in less than 24 hours was close to perfection. But not by her standards.

"I may have done it right, but I didn't do it perfectly," she says. "At 2,500 feet I fell. The sun hit the wall and I knew it was too hot to go on. I waited five hours for it to cool then let myself be talked into trying it again too soon. I actually fell a total of three times. Each time you fall, you have to start at the beginning of the pitch. Having to go over ground again can really take it out of you. I knew I was losing strength fast.

"But I did it in 23 hours, in one shot, from the ground up," she says. "The hardest part of this route was near the top after climbing over 2,000 feet. I needed to have not only endurance, but a considerable amount of power and concentration when I arrived at these sections. It would be like running a marathon at a seven-minute per mile pace, then suddenly increasing that pace to a five-minute mile toward the end. There was one spot there that I called Houdini, because it looked so improbable. I had to invent a technique that required a strange kind of contortion movement. At first I couldn't see any holes at all. That's where creative visualization comes in. You have to look at the features and forms of the rock and imagine a way of using them and adapting your body appropriately."

Not surprisingly, other climbers often try to figure out just why Lynn has been so successful and there's still a lot of talk on the web and in the press about just what factors led to the historic climb. "After I climbed The Nose," says Lynn, "a lot of guys said that I was able to do it simply because I had the advantage of small fingers. It's true that having small fingers was an advantage on one section. I have small fingers

Although retired from competition, Lynn Hill is still considered one of the most accomplished athletes of all time in her sport.

because I'm a small person. So, yes, that is one advantage. On the other hand, because I'm small, I have the disadvantage of not being able to do long reaches. There are advantages and disadvantages both ways. One tends to offset the other. Trying to make the long reaches for me would be like trying to play basketball with seven-footers.

"The point is that there aren't any secrets to climbing The Nose or doing anything else athletically. To be successful, you just have to have the necessary skill, training and vision in order to achieve your goals."

Many non-athletes or athletes who are just starting out assume that doing a sport like rock climbing is mostly about being strong. While, certainly being in shape is always a pre-requisite for an endurance sport like climbing, according to Lynn, a lot of what differentiates the successful from the unsuccessful effort is above the shoulders.

"Your state of mind is so important," says Lynn. "Climbing is a sport that involves you and the rock. The rock is a totally natural formation that's been there for maybe millions of years. When you're on the rock, you have no choice but to adapt to what is there. It may not be what you'd hoped was there or what you think should be there. The rock is indiffer-ent to gender, size or whatever you think it should be."

Like most very successful athletes, Lynn has found that it is a necessity to be able separate self-confidence from egotism.

"A climb is not an ego trip," says Lynn. "If you let your ego get in the way of what you're trying to do, you're done before you start. Egotism is a very self defeating emotion."

She also believes that an athlete must be able to follow her own instincts about what the right thing to do is in any given situation. "If you let other people talk you into things that you don't agree with, you can get in a lot of trouble," says Lynn. "When you're out there on the rock, you can't be hav-ing second thoughts. This is never the time to wonder if you're doing the right thing. You have to always be 'in the moment.' You have to concentrate totally on what you're doing. The time for the 'what ifs' is when you're back on the ground after the climb."

Obviously, in climbing, there is little margin for error. That's why Lynn feels that being aware of your body at all times is so important. "In a difficult climb being off just one millimeter can cause you to slip," says Lynn. "Your body positioning has to be very precise. You always have to be aware of where the center of your body is. It may look like climbers are always strung out all over the rock, but what you're always striving for is balance. Anytime you're off balance, you have to rely on strength. And if you are always relying on strength, you won't have the energy to get very far."

Much has been written about the differences in male and female physiology in relation to sports performance. Experts have endlessly analyzed the advantages women have in being blessed with a greater percentage of slow-twitch muscle and greater flexibility. There have been studies about what impact the smaller joints that women have may be. There is even speculation that the fact that women have wider hips and smaller skeletons is important. While she doesn't deny that these differences exist, Lynn believes that in most cases, balance is really the issue. "It's all about physics," she says.

Although each rock face presents its own set of challenges, Lynn has found that years of experience have prepared her for most situations. "After 26 years, you get so you can memorize the sequence of when you should do things," she says. "Even if I've never been to a place before, now I know pretty well where to look for a hold. It gets to be intuitive. To the average person, that rock face may look absolutely smooth, like it doesn't have even one crack it, but if you know where and how to look, you can find them. Experience gives you a balance between what you can consciously see and what you intuitively know."

To many, rock climbing would seem like the ultimate high-stress experience. Lynn finds it to be just the opposite. "Because climbing requires so much focus, it provides a temporary escape from the other parts of your life," she says.

"When you're up there climbing, all you should be thinking about is that rock. You should concentrate completely on what moves you need to make next and what your objective should be."

Another thing that attracts Lynn to the sport is the utter simplicity of climbing. "Obviously, climbing serves no practical purpose," she says. "But it provides very meaningful experiences. Some sports are very contrived. The natural environment has been altered in such a way that you don't have to exert much effort. Climbing is just the opposite. It's all about learning to adapt totally to the environment you're in. I think it provides the perfect opportunity for learning about what makes you tick. When you're that involved in the external world, you can really explore your inner nature."

Although Lynn prefers free climbing, occasionally she's tried some of the other variations of the sport. Well, most of them. "I would never want to free solo," she says. "Free soloing is climbing without any kind of safety rope. For me, it's not worth the risk of getting killed or injured," she says. "One little slip and what ends up on the ground would not be pretty."

Some climbers use their ropes and gear to essentially haul themselves up. "I've never been much attracted to that," says Lynn. "I prefer the challenge and freedom of free climbing."

Bouldering does offer some attraction to her. "Bouldering is a real social form of climbing," she says. "What you do is go out to these big fields of boulders and take along a mat to land on if you fall. There's a great place to do this in Fountainbleau, France. The boulders are in this sandy area, so you would have a comparatively soft landing. It's in a beautiful setting. I think people are attracted to bouldering because it's like a game of chess. Each section presents its own challenges. The pieces are your body. The challenge is finding a way to climb up the most difficult section of rock imaginable."

Most experienced climbers develop a preference for particular types of rock formations. "I particularly like overhanging features," says Lynn. "When you climb up a vertical rock face, you're thinking two-dimensionally. When you do an overhang, you have to think three-dimensionally—up, out and sideways. Free climbing The Nose required a variety of techniques from low angle slab climbing, to crack climbing, to vertical face climbing. The most spectacular overhanging section was at the very end."

Many climbers describe climbing in terms of conquering the rock. Lynn rejects that theory. "Climbing is less about conquering and more about finding harmony between myself and the environment," she says. "I guess to some, it does require strength, which is considered a very masculine quality. But it is just as much about grace and flexibility. I would describe the skills necessary for a climber as being more like water—strong but soft. To me, it's always about yielding to the rock. Looking for ways you can be in harmony with what you're trying to do. The rock is relatively unchanging. It's up to me to adapt to it."

Just as Kim McKnight has found that through visual projection she can now easily find her way down a mountain, even in the midst of a blinding snowstorm, Lynn uses visualization to see where the route she has chosen is going. "You usually can't see much of what's coming up other than maybe a broad overall perspective," she says. "But you can and should work two to three moves in advance. You think about which hand to put where. Then you look at the next hold.

Your goal is always to have three points of contact on the rock. That might be two hands and one foot or two feet and one hand. That's what keeps your body in balance and keeps you from having to rely on strength alone to get you to the next place."

"I would compare how I move to how a billiards player plays," says Lynn. "You're focusing on the move you're about to make, but, at the same time, you're always thinking ahead several moves. Each move you make helps set you up for the next one. Your hands and feet work in a push and pull sequence so you need to know not just where to find the holds, but what features will provide the best combination of moves to get you where you want to go."

Again, visualizing is essential. "You have to imagine where you're going," says Lynn. "You want your body to flow up the rock in a smooth motion. If you're jerking and grabbing and falling out of balance, you're going to use up a lot of energy you may need later. You need to be aware of where the center of your body is at all times. It just takes experience to be able to recognize which features of the rock can help you do that."

Athletes like DeeDee Jonrowe, Heather Hedrick and Kristen Lignell must push on, regardless of the weather. Lynn says that she doesn't see rock climbing like that. "Rain, snow or extreme heat provide too dangerous a situation," says Lynn. "When it starts doing one of those things, I get off the rock as soon as possible. If the rock is wet, it's too easy to slip and lose your footing. If the rock is too hot, and you sweat too much, you can't grip the rock properly. I just have no desire to freeze my fingers or my feet. If I were climbing a snow-covered mountain, I suppose I would wear gloves. But for technical rock climbing that would be like putting boots on a gymnast."

"Obviously, I don't perform gymnastics like I used to," says Lynn. "Gymnastics is a sport that favors the immature body. The best gymnasts are still little girls. I may not have the range of motion I did when I was a kid, but through running, yoga and a lot of stretching, I'm still very flexible. I like to ski, snowboard and surf, although I'll admit I don't like being cold very much. I've done a lot of sports in my day, and I'll probably do a lot more, but climbing will always be my favorite."

Like many professional athletes, Lynn has had her sponsors, among others North Face, Petzl, Beal and LaSportiva. And like Sarah Fisher and DeeDee Jonrowe, sponsorship has involved making appearances, signing autographs and doing public speaking. Such activities have inevitably taken time away from practice and competition, but like other women athletes, Lynn has accepted the responsibility. "Their support makes it possible for me to pursue the sport I love," she says. "It's a give and take relationship."

During her career, Lynn has competed in both the United States and abroad. "I used to compete in Europe, France and Italy," she says. This competition provided an unexpected benefit. "When I was in Europe I found that learning a language was a lot like climbing," she says. "You start by studying the basics, learning the grammar and how each part of the sentence goes together. You pay close attention to pronunciation. Then you listen and learn how to make the language flow. To me it was a lot like learning a sport. At first you are clumsy with it. You sound a lot like a child. But if you make yourself get around those who do it well and keep trying, eventually you'll get it right. If you're timid or give up, you'll never get anywhere."

Although Lynn has done some coaching, currently she is focusing on writing a book that she hopes to have completed in 2001. "I consider this book fragments of my autobiography," she says, "but mainly it is about the development of the sport, some of my experiences as a climber and how these events helped shape the person I have become."

In addition to working on the book, Lynn plans to continue to climb and to travel some. "I'll climb some here in Colorado where I live," she says. "Then, I'm thinking seriously about the Legend competition in Italy in May for the "X" masters of this competition in the late 1980s and early 1900s. I don't compete anymore, but I'll participate in this event as kind of a celebration. This competition in Arco is known as the Wimbleton of free climbing. All the people from the early days will be there and it should be a lot of fun."

When she comes back, there will be more sponsor appearances for North Face.

"Now that I'm 40, climbing is not the same for me as it was when I was 25," she says. "But for me, there is still always that next challenge, that next level of mastery. I know I am both physically and mentally different than I was when I was younger. Age may have changed how I can approach climbing, but all my experiences have given me the ability to look deeper within and do more with less."

"After all," says Lynn, "Climbing is not about reaching the top, it's about how you get there."

5

Dream Big and Dare to Fail

A Profile of DeeDee Jonrowe—Musher

Alaska's Iditarod is often called "The Last Great Race on Earth," and it's easy to see why. The 1,100-mile race that begins in downtown Anchorage and ends in Nome, covers mountainous terrain, and is generally held in frigid weather and blinding snowstorms.

Like the modern marathon, the Iditarod commemorates a historic event. In 1925, a diphtheria epidemic broke out in Nome. Located on the banks of the Bering Sea, and cut off from shipping lanes by pack ice, the city was 1,000 miles from Anchorage and the nearest diphtheria serum. Although the Alaska Railroad was able to take the serum as far as Nenana — 250 miles north of Anchorage—the lifesaving task of getting it the rest of the way fell to 20 volunteers who loaded it onto their dog sleds and carried it the rest of the way. At one point the sled carrying the serum was overturned and the musher had to dig the serum out of the snow with his bare hands, but it arrived in Nome in five days and seven hours and the town was saved.

Although to most people dog sledding seems extremely exotic, the use of dogs to pull sleds is hardly new to the people who live near the Arctic Circle. Archeological evidence sug-

gests that native peoples used sled dogs as early as 4,000 years ago. Dog sledding as a recreational activity may have existed nearly that long although the first written account of a formal race documents a race from Winnipeg to St. Paul, Minnesota in the 1850s. Some thirty years later, in 1886, dog sled races were featured in the first St. Paul Winter Carnival, where they are held to this day.

During the Gold Rush, the All-Alaska Sweepstakes were organized by Scotty Allan, who was a horse trader. During the 1920s sled dog racing is said to have enjoyed popularity in New England, as well.

In 1932, sled dog racing was included in the first Winter Olympics held in North America (Lake Placid, New York). This event consisted of seven-dog teams running 25 miles a day for two days. Dog sleds were also a part of the 1952 Oslo Olympics, although they were used in pulka races, an event in which the driver follows the dogs on skis behind a pulka (toboggan).

The use of sled dogs for transportation in Alaska was gradually supplanted by aircraft and snowmobiles during the 1950s and 1960s, however interest in the sport has been maintained largely through the internationally known Iditarod, started in 1967. The first Iditarod was hardly the grueling event it is today. Only 27 miles long, it covered a small section of the current Iditarod Trail. Gradually, through the work of promoters like Joe Redington, the event grew in both popularity and notoriety. In 1992, the International Federation of Sleddog Sports was founded to promote the sport both nationally and internationally. Although many other dog races are held each year, the Iditarod has remained the most famous of all.

Today, the Iditarod attracts dozens of men and women and

thousands of dogs to compete in the annual event that follows one of two courses, a northern course in even-numbered years and a southern course in odd-numbered years.

* * *

On March 15, 1998, to the cheers of thousands of fans gathered for the event, DeeDee Jonrowe's team of dogs, pulled her sled across the finish line in Nome, Alaska to complete the Iditarod, known to dog sled racing enthusiasts around the world as The Last Great Race on Earth. The race had been a long one. For nine days, eight hours, twenty-six minutes and ten seconds she had coaxed and cajoled a team of Alaskan Huskies across 1,100 miles of rugged, snow covered, mountain terrain. But for that moment, at least, the dark and the cold and the aching muscles of the last week and a half were forgotten. After 18 years of competition, DeeDee had matched her best finish ever, coming in second, just minutes behind the winner.

To the many fans who had faithfully followed her career, the spectacular second place finish was no surprise. For the past 10 years, she had finished in the top ten every year—six times, counting this one, in the top five. This race was the second time she had placed second.

Unlike many of her fellow competitors, DeeDee hadn't grown up in the sport. In fact for most of her growing up years, she hadn't even lived in the US. She was born in Germany in 1953 while her father was in the service there, and, like a lot of other Army brats, DeeDee moved 20 times in 22 years. Her first school experience was in Ethiopia, about as far away from the snowy peaks of Alaska as you can get. Her middle school years were spent in Okinawa. It wasn't until she was in high school that the family finally settled for a few years in Virginia, then moved to Anchorage.

In 1971, DeeDee entered the University of Alaska at Fairbanks majoring in wildlife management. After graduation in 1974, she went to work for the Alaska Department of Fish and Game and was sent to Bethel, a predominately Eskimo community—population 2,500—quite literally out in the middle of nowhere. Although there was certainly no shortage of dogs in Bethel, it wasn't until her city league basketball team was in Nome to compete in a tournament that she saw Rick Swenson win the Iditarod. She knew then that that was something she had to try. In 1977 she married co-worker Mike Jonrowe and the couple started buying dogs. By 1979, they had 20 dogs and the next year DeeDee entered her first Iditarod.

Today, DeeDee, husband Mike and 100 or so dogs live in Willow, 75 miles north of Anchorage where, in addition to training year round, they operate a kennel.

"I've always loved dogs," says DeeDee. "As a kid, anytime I saw a dog, I'd immediately drop to my knees to play with it. Then, when I got older and moved to Alaska, I saw the opportunity to help these dogs do what they intuitively want to do. I first got into competition for this reason, then I got hooked on it. These dogs are unbelievable, they're just crazy to go all the time. They're driven to want to do this. Now, I'm probably as driven as they are. I pretty much share my whole life with them."

Although she formed an immediate enthusiasm for the sport, she didn't actually know much about it. "I bought my first five dogs from this guy, but since I lived 400 miles away in an Eskimo community, we didn't have any contact after that," she says. "The Eskimos in Bethel had been around dogs all their lives and knew what they were doing, but in their culture, it is really rude to ask a lot of questions, especially if you're a white woman. I pretty much taught myself to race by watching what they did and just taking my cues from the dogs."

When DeeDee first started racing, very few women had ever competed but to DeeDee being one of the only women was never her motivation. "It's my bond with the dogs that keeps me in this sport," she says. "I hardly ever think about the fact that I've always been one of the few women. Everyone has some advantages and disadvantages in this race. That's what is so way cool about it. You have to train to accentuate your strengths and minimize your weaknesses. In comparison to men, my size is a distinct advantage, but my upper body development compared to theirs is a weakness. So I just try not to get into situations where I would need to manhandle my way out of it. I've never been impressed by women who try to manipulate men to do their part. I would never want to get to Nome because some man had to babysit me. I've seen that kind of thing happen on the Eco-Challenge where women use their wiles to overcome lack of preparation. In this sport, I can honestly say I'm not treated any differently than the men. In general, you're treated like you treat other people. If you're pathetic, people will treat you that way. You should be responsible for yourself."

While there is nothing to stop women from entering the race, the number of women who do has not increased much over the years. "I'd say the number of competent women has actually decreased," says DeeDee. "You have to remember that there really are only about 30 people capable of finishing in the top 20 positions and about 10 who have a chance to win. This isn't a race that you can win the first time you try. Since Susan Butcher retired, there are really no comparable female competitors. This is a very demanding sport. Most women are just not strong enough. This isn't something every woman can do."

When DeeDee was first getting started she entered a few local races but found them unsatisfying. "When you know what these dogs can do, you want to be in an event that really takes advantage of their strength and endurance," she says. "Also, like the dogs, I like something that is a real adventure, something that puts me out there on the edge."

Not surprisingly, preparing for a race as grueling as the Iditarod, takes a lot of training. Although for years, practicing with the dogs provided enough physical conditioning, recently DeeDee began a weight training program, as well. "When you do any sport for 20 years, eventually it takes a toll on your body," says DeeDee. "I've had back surgery, frozen my shoulder, broken my hand and four years ago was in an auto accident that resulted in serious abdominal surgery. When your body has been through these kinds of things, it takes a professional trainer to work with you to address these issues."

In addition to weight lifting, six years ago DeeDee started running. "I started running mainly because I wanted to understand what the dogs were going through," she says. "Then, I got hooked on that sport, as well. So far I've competed in four marathons, each a 28 mile endurance race that, although not exactly an ultra marathon, does require running four miles up a mountain, through rivers, glaciers and whatever else is on the trail. I don't consider myself a great runner. I run with a group of friends and try to hike or climb at least three times a week. It's great and I love it, but I'll admit that it's a humbling experience to be at the top of one sport and then try another."

Not surprisingly, when she runs, there is often a dog along.

While many athletes devote basically all their spare time to personal conditioning, in dog sledding, that is simply not an option.

"My personal trainer thinks I should work out more, but in this sport you just don't have the time to do training more than one day a week," says DeeDee. "This sport is all about the dogs and that takes a lot of time. Typically, I'll get up, water and feed the dogs, then hook up one team and go out for 30 miles. I come back and have lunch and start the same routine with the second team. Then on the weekends, I may drive 400 miles to a race. Often that means that I may be either racing or training eight or nine days in a row and that leaves me pretty beat up. I can't just think about myself in this sport. When you have 37 dogs to care for, by the end of the day, you're pretty tired. "

While it would certainly be possible to assign at least some of the care of the dogs to someone else, DeeDee believes that the ongoing connection the racer has with the dogs is vital.

"There's nothing that happens to these dogs that I'm not involved in," she says. "The time you spend bonding with the dogs is just as valuable as the training. The fact that the dogs are bonded with you is part of their motivation to succeed. Sometimes I'll just go out and sit on their doghouse and play around with them. That's never wasting time. When you put that kind of effort into them, they'll reward you by giving back to you. That's the real reason why this sport is so important to me. It would have to be for me to be so passionate about it for 20 years."

"In summer, dogs are fed once a day and watered twice," she says. "In winter I feed them three times a day, sometimes four, depending on how cold it is. In the fall, I train the dogs for power and by winter they're as strong as strong can be. And that's really tough training. When we train, we don't have a nice groomed course. When there's not much snow we're running over roots and in the trees, we're bumping and thumping a lot of the time. It's easy to catch a runner and get all out of balance so there's a lot of jarring and banging going on. And, like maybe mountain biking, everything is happening really fast, so you don't have time to anticipate and avoid stuff. The dogs are really individuals and like all individuals, they have their good days and their bad days," she says. "So some practice runs and some races are bound to go better than others."

In addition to training around Willow, DeeDee has found that she needs to take the dogs to other parts of the state, as well.

"We train everywhere," says DeeDee. "You have to expose

the dogs to all the kinds of conditions they will encounter during a race. Last year, for example, we flew the dogs to Nome to get them used to the wind. Here in central Alaska, there isn't much wind and these dogs aren't used to the noise and feel of it. If they haven't been in wind much, they'll really be spooked by it. I found that out the hard way in the 1999 race when I had to pull off the course."

Like most sports, racing sled dogs demands a good deal of personal sacrifice. "There's personal sacrifice in any sport," says DeeDee. "But in this sport, you can't ever get away from it for even a few days. The dogs are depending on you and they want you to be there for them all the time. A lot of people look at this and all they see is the fun part of it, but when they try it they find out that hard work sets in. For months and months at a time there is no glamour to it. You spend a lot of time in the mud and in the rain and you never graduate from shoveling poop. It's one thing to have to make yourself do another rep or two, but it's quite another thing to shovel a dog yard day after day. You have to be real motivated to do that."

In addition to time, DeeDee also has a significant financial investment in the dogs. "This sport is expensive," she says. "I spend every dime I have on it and I could always spend more for more wood chips for the dog yard or something like that. At Christmas, I spent $250 on big knucklebones for the dogs because I knew they'd like that. Your budget is pretty much determined by what you have."

It takes about $300 per year per dog counting the cost of food and vaccinations and other expenses. Then there are the costs of entering races. The entry fee for the Iditarod, for example, is $1,750 and the award for first prize is just $62,000. Added to that is the cost of shipping the dogs not just to other places in Alaska but also to Europe, where DeeDee also participates in the Alpirod, a 600-mile long dog sled race through the countryside of France, Switzerland, Italy and Austria.

"It might be cheaper to buy a dog, as opposed to raising them," says DeeDee even though a good leader can cost up to $5,000. "But a dog that someone was willing to sell wouldn't make my team. If someone was willing to sell it that would probably mean that there was a problem I wouldn't want."

An investment in a dog is a long term one.

"Dogs aren't like a bike or a pair of skis," says DeeDee. "They aren't machinery. Dogs are very independent. They want to work for one person and even then it takes time to get them to want to work for you. It can easily take a year for a dog to want to do that. The leaders, especially, demand your respect. If a dog doesn't respect you, you aren't going to get anywhere. That's why I do everything for my dogs. I want to be connected to everything they like. Raising a dog is a different game. It is a long-term relationship that takes a lot of patience. There always comes a point when you can begin to see what the future of a dog could be. You can see that it has the potential to be awesome. But you have to go at this one step at a time. You can't let a dog get in over his head. You can't let him fail. I think my strength is an innate ability to sense what a dog needs and what to do with him. Anyone can harness them up and even train them to stand beside each other, but beyond that you have to know how to develop them. I love it, but I'm always very involved."

The dogs that DeeDee races are Alaskan Huskies, specially bred for this sport. "These aren't an AKC breed," she says. "These are the descendants of the dogs that carried the mail and hauled the gold. They aren't bred for their looks. They're bred for function. Show dogs, by comparison are bred for looks, so breeders will often repeat genetic weaknesses like thyroid problems and hip displaysia in order to get the look they want. I think that is just wrong. We pay careful attention to genetics. I'll race a dog with a genetic problem, but will neuter him and not let him breed. For example, I've dedicated nine years to an epileptic dog."

DeeDee feels strongly enough about this issue that she has become active in a campaign for responsible breeding. And, certainly by now, she knows as much about Huskies as just about anybody.

"You have to start working with the dogs as pups," she says. "One of the first things you let them know is that fighting is not tolerated. If they start that, you pick them up. Once their feet are off the ground they realize they're helpless. You look them in the eye to get their attention and firmly say, 'NO!' If they start to do unacceptable things like chew the lines, I pick them up and shake them. They get the idea."

When dogs can no longer race, many go on to a second career. "A dog that doesn't race anymore is my best training tool," says DeeDee. "They become behavior examples to puppies and yearlings. Dogs at any age love to go, even if they can only go four miles. But they set an example for the younger dogs. They do the discipline for you.

"Huskies are so trainable, any thing you try to teach them they learn 150%. They are bred to be work dogs so you have to keep them busy. In fact, they just have so much zeal, you have to be careful what you teach them to do. They've always got places to go and things to do. People who buy them as pets and don't give them enough exercise are usually in for an unpleasant surprise. If the dogs don't have enough to do, they'll start thinking things up and sometimes those things can be pretty destructive.

"They have an independent streak in them, too," says DeeDee. "If they get away, they can be gone an hour to an hour and a half and you could never catch them. They're cute, but they're not stuffed animals. A lot of them get taken back to the pound. But if you do take the time with them, they are just so much fun."

In many professions, like police work, it is important that dogs be regarded as working partners and not pets. Sled dogs are different.

"They can't really help but be pets," says DeeDee. "By the time they're ready to race, you've spent time camping with them and sleeping with them and you know each other pretty well. They have to respect you which means that you have to be around them a lot. Their life depends on you so you have to give their development your full time attention. You have to be consistent with them and discipline them—just like kids. You can love them, but you can't let emotion drive a dog team."

Although sled dogs tend to have distinct and strong personalities, they function extremely well as a team.

"The easiest thing about our dogs is that they have always been together," says DeeDee, "so they gravitate toward a group. They don't want to be alone. Dogs are social animals. If you act confident and make reasonable demands, they'll do what you ask."

DeeDee admits, however, that there is more than one way to raise a sled dog.

*For more than 20 years, Dee Dee Jonrowe has been one of the few women to finish
the 1,100-mile Iditarod race across Alaska.*

"Unlike me, some guys are very quiet with their dogs. They don't talk to them or touch them much. And that seems to work for them. I'm different. I love to play with them. When we're out on the trail and we stop to rest, we'll play, too. That's what my dogs are used to."

As in any sport, over the years there has been a certain amount of controversy focused on whether an endurance competition like the Iditarod is harmful to the dogs.

"If dogs are well cared for and well trained, racing doesn't pose much of a health risk to sled dogs," says DeeDee. "Since racing is a competition and the dogs are competitors, of course there is a chance they can be injured. In this race, the most common injuries are to the dog's shoulder or wrist."

In the event that one of her dogs is injured, "I would immediately pull him out of the race, put him in a sled bag and send him home," says DeeDee. "I also pay very close attention to every dog to try to spot signs that an injury may be developing. I can usually tell how a dog feels by the way he holds his ears. I also study the urine. If urine is brown, I know that the dog has muscle soreness that could turn into an injury."

Although an injury means an automatic trip home, it isn't the only reason DeeDee will take a dog out of the race. "If a dog isn't having fun, I'll send him back home," she says. "If he doesn't want to be in this race, I don't want him to have to be there."

Rarely, but occasionally a dog does die during a race and there is always a lot of publicity. However, every precaution is taken to prevent a fatality. There are 36 veterinarians on the course, at least two at each check point and all vets carry notebooks with the running record of each dog.

"You have to remember that there are 1,000 dogs in this race," says DeeDee. In any city with that many dogs, on any given day, there would probably be at least one dog death. No one thinks anything about that."

Dogs aren't the only athletes in the race, however. The race can take its toll on the humans, too, and DeeDee has suffered her share of injuries. During the Iditarod she sleeps with the team on the sled. "I give the dogs 12 hours of rest per 24. But because I have so much to do, I usually get no more than four hours.

"I think I've had every single cold related injury," says DeeDee. "I haven't had any amputations, but I have had severe frostbite on my fingers, cheeks and nose. I even frost-bit my corneas some years ago, so now I have to be very care-ful. By far the most serious problem I had in the cold was hypothermia. Ironically, it wasn't even on a race. I'd taken a woman friend out for what was supposed to be just a short afternoon ride and we got caught in a snowstorm. For three days we had to wait it out in a tent. Because we only thought we'd be out for the afternoon, we hadn't packed matches, food or water. Before long, we were both suffering from hypother-mia. And believe me, this is not what you see in the movies. With hypothermia, you don't just gradually fade into a peace-ful sleep. At times I would shiver so hard that my diaphragm would seize up. When the storm was over we let the dogs go so that they could find their way back to camp. I crawled back because I was too weak to walk. It was by far my worst training experience. The other woman is still suffering the side effects. I guess it's like that old saying, 'What doesn't kill you makes you stronger.'"

Although the hypothermia was DeeDee's most frightening training injury, much worse by far was an automobile acci-

dent in 1996 which involved DeeDee, Mike, and her grandmother.

"The accident was quite honestly the worst thing that ever
happened to me," says DeeDee. "We were trapped in the car
and there was nothing I could do for my grandmother but
watch her die. Mike actually did basically die at one point
and all I could do was pray that he could be brought back,
which, fortunately, he was. After that, I haven't worried
about injury again. So I break a leg? So what? Nothing
could be worse than that accident. Now, the only thing I still
fear is injury to a dog because they totally depend on me.

"But this brings up a very important thing about races like
the Iditarod," says DeeDee. "Actually, training can be far
more dangerous than being in a race. In a race, you are
required to carry a certain amount of survival gear plus people know you're out there and if you don't show up, they'll
start looking for you."

In addition to the weather, because training occurs in the
wilderness, there are other hazards to consider as well, like
large and potentially dangerous animals.

"I carry a gun," says DeeDee, although she admits that
solving one problem in this area sometimes creates another.

"I have killed a moose," she says, "but that's the last thing I
ever would want to do. A dead animal in the midst of a dog
team creates a huge commotion and a huge mess. It's also a
big hassle. If you shoot one, you have to gut it for human
consumption then call the state troopers to come and get it."

Like most athletes, DeeDee has found that she needs to
pay attention to her diet.

"Diet is important in any sport and obviously differs considerably from sport to sport," says DeeDee. "I can see a big difference between what I need for running and what I need for racing. When I run, for example, quantity is important. You can only tolerate just so much jostling around in your stomach. Generally I try to achieve a good balance between protein and fat, but other than that don't do much that's special. I spend a lot more time thinking about dog food. As for me, I'm much more likely to be concerned about what I can carry that is convenient and won't freeze. So within that limitation, I try to take along things like peanut butter sandwiches and dried salmon—things that I can eat easily and that taste good.

Like auto racing, skydiving and mountaineering, competition in dog sledding involves a certain amount of gear.

"Obviously the sled is a very important piece of equipment," says DeeDee. "The sleds we use now are flexible, and made out of materials a lot like cross country skis. In addition, we have to carry survival food, snowshoes, an ax, booties for the dogs' feet, a cooker, dog food and sleeping bags. The sled and gear together generally weigh from 100-120 lbs. Another really important piece of gear is the headlamp. I spend a lot of time with the lamp on, so it's important to have one that is really dependable."

Not surprisingly, clothing is an important consideration in this sport.

"Basically I want it to be as light as possible," says DeeDee. "Eddie Bauer is my sponsor and I rely on their expertise in this area. They custom make all the stuff I wear. They've been studying me for 20 years and in that time there have been significant changes in fabrics. Because of both the cold and the time I'll be wearing the clothes, I'll generally have on six layers. What makes all this difficult to get right is that what I do isn't consistent throughout the race. Cross country skiers, for example, need clothes that aren't so warm, because they basically are exerting themselves all the time. Snowboarders may need warmer clothing, because they are sedentary a lot of the time. I may have to sprint up the side of a mountain and then stand still in a 100 mph wind. So I need layers for insulation, but also need fabrics that will per-form quickly and wick moisture. Yet at the same time, I can't be so bundled up that if something goes wrong, I can't have the flexibility I need to fix the sled or disentangle a dog. Also, I can't ever put any piece of clothing down. If I stop to fix something on the sled and the dogs decide to take off, there's no going back. That's why I keep my mittens on a string around my neck, just like little kids do."

In formal racing events like the Iditarod, there are very specific regulations about what gear DeeDee and the other racers can and can't carry.

"In many ways, we race pretty much the same as the way the Eskimos did hundreds of years ago," says DeeDee. "We can't, for example, put sails on the sleds. Remember, the Eskimos raced the sleds that they used for other things, and their sleds were all wooden and certainly a lot stiffer than what we use for racing, now. Sleds like that would certainly have the advantage of being very sturdy, but they can't wiggle through trails and squeeze through tight places. We have to go through everything, so we have to look for a sled that is both flexible and sturdy enough to take a big whacking from time to time. This is a very long course, and understandably, people didn't want to have to make the parts through the trees any wider than necessary. Sometimes, on a really skinny section, you can literally get stuck. You may even have to detach the dogs and tie them to a tree while you bring the sled around."

Because the race lasts such a long time, racers don't even try to carry all the provisions they'll need with them at all times.

"At the beginning of the race, you have to take all the food, yours and the dogs', to the race committee and they take possession of it," says DeeDee. "Once you do that, you can't add or subtract what you gave them."

Although the race committee is supposed to deposit it in corrals along the way, according to DeeDee, planning is one thing, execution another. "I've gotten to a corral and found it completely empty," she says. "Other times wolves have gotten to my stuff. Now, I always carry emergency supplies."

Even the best preparation, however can leave a racer stranded without some necessary gear. At times like that, most find that they need to depend on the good will of a fellow competitor.

"One time I completely ran out of batteries for my head-lamp," says DeeDee. "I had to make a deal with the next competitor that came along. If he'd loan me some batteries, I promised I wouldn't pass him. And I didn't. When you're out there for 10 days, you have to depend on each other and trust each other. You have to be as good as your word."

Although some of the rules of the race are fairly specific, in one very important area, the rules are surprisingly flexible. A musher must start with 12 dogs and finish with five, but other than that the number of dogs on the team is pretty much up to the competitor.

"It may seem like the more dogs you have, the better off you are," says DeeDee, "but a sled team is only as fast as the slowest dog. And every race is different. I've sent dogs home for different reasons, sometimes as many as three. Sometimes it's just easier to care for fewer dogs. The more dogs you have, the more time you have to spend taking care of them. And the more time you spend, the less time you have for sleep. You can get worn down pretty fast. Also, sometimes, for a variety of reasons, a dog just gets overwhelmed. My philosophy is that if the dog isn't having fun, he should go home. Each of these dogs has a career in this sport, just like me. And you don't gain anything by forcing them to do something they don't want to do."

Like auto racing, sponsorship is an important factor in the Iditarod.

"Sponsorship in this sport generally has to be earned. I've placed in the top ten in this race without a sponsor. Once I proved myself, they came to me. Now I have significant sponsorship. Sponsorship is very much a two-way deal. The way I see it, I have an obligation to show them what I can do for them. That means when I accept sponsorship support, I'll be willing to do the appearances, do motivational speaking, test gear – whatever. Obviously, I'm a great one for testing gear. I actually wear those boots 18 hours a day and that parka for 10 days in the worst weather imaginable. In addition, I've been doing some testing for Microsoft. For years, we've kept very detailed records about our business. In addition to the usual financial records, we've kept all the details about genetics, blood lines, medical records, heat cycles, whelping reports, blood analyses and on and on. We also keep careful records about food. We change the diets of the dogs a lot, depending on what season it is and what they're doing. For example, in the summer, a dog may need only around 1,200 calories. When a dog's in training, that number goes up to around 3,600 and when we're racing, a dog may consume as many as 10,000 to 15,000 calories a day. We rely on our records to know what we need for each dog. It turns out that the records involved in our business were very complex. It surprised the software people."

In addition to attracting sponsors, DeeDee has also gained a large and loyal following, including a lot of kids. While she thinks it is especially important to respond to them, usually there just isn't time.

"It's hard to communicate with them they way I'd like," she says. "I don't have a press secretary or PR staff. It's hard to spend much time writing letters when you're out shoveling dog poop. I used to have a neighbor who helped with the mail from kids. When she moved away, the local senior center called and asked if they could help. So I asked them if they'd like to take over answering the kids' mail. I get about 3,000 letters a year, so it's no small task, but they seem to enjoy it. I try to get over there and talk with them and have dinner with them as often as I can to say thanks."

Although DeeDee would be the first to admit that her sport, by nature, is a solitary one, still, just as she realizes that the dogs need emotional support, so too, does she.

"The emotional support of my family is what keeps me going," says DeeDee. "I feel like they always deserve my best effort. They've been the reason I've stayed in racing."

"The biggest psychological advantage I have is my faith. I believe God gives me the ability to live on the edge like I do, to take me out of the comfort zone. At the same time, God also gives me the ability to fall on my face sometimes but get up and go back at it. Salvation has noting to do with physical ability. The dogs have given me a picture of God's unconditional love. The dogs love me no matter what I do. That reminds me of how God loves me."

In addition to her religious faith, Dee Dee has always been inspired by arctic explorer Colonel Normal Vaughn, who at age 94, is the oldest living survivor of Admiral Byrd's expedition. "He's just amazing," says DeeDee, noting that just this year he drove a snowmobile more than 800 miles by himself in a reenactment of the 1925 Serum Run. "His slogan is 'Dream big and dare to fail.' I guess you could say that's pretty much my personal philosophy, too.

"This sport is certainly doable. I've done it for all these years, but when people come to me for advice about getting started in it, I want to be very clear to them what is involved. I don't want to set anyone up to fail. A thirst for adventure is not enough in this sport. You have to be primarily motivated by the love of dogs. This is a dog race, not a people race and you can get dogs into big trouble because of your ego. Just because you were an accomplished athlete in another sport, doesn't mean you will be good at this."

In her book, *Iditarod Dreams*, DeeDee summed it up this way: "If winning is the only reason you are out on the Iditarod Trail, then you are going to be disappointed for many, many years. If your goal is to do your best and be a positive influence in people's lives, then you can be a winner every year."

6
Snow, Wind and Thin Air

A Profile of Kristen Lignell—Mountaineer

Although certainly women must have been climbing mountains right along with men before recorded history, the first documented climb by a woman was of a Miss Parminter who allegedly scaled the Alps along with her male companion in 1799. In the early 1800s another French woman, Marie Paradis, successfully climbed Mont Blanc and in the 1880s Meta Brevoot and Lucy Walker made history by shedding their skirts and replacing them with trousers which they thought, not surprisingly, would be just a little easier to climb in. Lucy is also said to have raised a few eyebrows when she disclosed that her training diet consisted largely of sponge cake, champagne and Asti Spumante. Despite her dubious nutritional regimen, in 1871 she nonetheless became the first woman to attempt the Matterhorn.

Annie Peck, who climbed the Matterhorn at age 44 is perhaps best known for her climbing-related feminist statement. On reaching the summit of a Peruvian mountain, she planted a flag that read, "Votes for Women."

By the 1920s, even though it was still largely dominated by men, mountaineering began to achieve some popularity among women. Mirium O'Brien, whose husband was also a climber, was perhaps the most famous of her time. In 1947, Barbara Washborn became the first woman to summit Denali (Mt.

McKinley) and in the 1950s, Bonnie Prudden made the news by climbing the Matterhorn with her new husband on their honeymoon. On May 16, 1976, the first all woman team (a team of Japanese women) became the first to reach the top of Mount Everest.

In the US, Denali is considered the ultimate challenge. In the early 1900s, the first explorers attempted to summit the mysterious mountain that they could see from their mining camps near Anchorage. By the 1930s, bush pilots were flying adventurers to the mountain's base camps and in 1954, the first commercial flight to Kahiltna Glacier gave climbers easy access to what, for most, is the starting point for their ascent.

Although it is now more accessible that it was in the early days, Denali is no less dangerous. Above 10,000 feet storms often drop the wind chill to 100 degrees year round and even the most experienced mountaineers find themselves gasping for breath at altitudes reaching well above 20,000 feet. Fewer than 50% of the people who start up the mountain reach the top. And each year the mountain, majestic and icy, claims the lives of some of those who dare to try.

*   *   *

When she was just four years old, Kristen Lignell's parents strapped her onto a pair of skis and before she even went to kindergarten, she was racing her brothers down the rolling hills of northern Michigan. Before long, it was hard to keep her in the house. "Some parents push their kids into sports," says Kristen. "But I can honestly say that wasn't the case with me. All they did was take me outside, show me what to do and encourage me to, above all, enjoy myself. Since it's winter at least eight months of the year in northern Michigan, a lot of what I ended up doing involved snow and ice."

Although she always loved to compete and even got to be very good, sports, for a girl growing up in the Midwest in the 1970s and 1980s, could, at best, be considered nothing more than a serious hobby. Even in the 1980s, a woman still needed a "real" career.

So off she went to the University of Michigan and four years later emerged as Kristen Lignell, R.N. While she had no doubt she'd eventually use her degree—after all, it's not easy to ignore that Midwestern work ethic—the quest for adventure won out over starting work immediately. The summer after graduation, she traded her nurse's cap for a backpack and spent a year traveling around Europe by herself. "It was a pivotal experience for me," says Kristen. "I'm the kind of person who is always on a mission. I knew that from that point on my dream would be to combine my love for adventure with a strong desire to learn about other cultures."

The question was how to afford to do both. Like many young women her age, the idea of adventure did not include moving back to her hometown and settling down. Instead, she headed west, landing in Squaw Valley, California. "Most people see a place like Squaw Valley only as a resort, a place to visit for a week at most," says Kristen. "But in reality, for the people who actually live here, it's really just a small town where basically everyone knows everyone else. We even call it Squawlywood. We strive for a high quality of life here in Lake Tahoe. Word tends to get around.

"At first my friends at Squaw Valley couldn't believe I could have learned to ski in Michigan," she says. "To them 500 vertical feet is nothing. But it's certainly enough to learn the basics on. We also did a lot of racing when I was growing up and that provided a solid background for me when I got to the powder, the chutes and the big bowls the western mountains have. I did OK."

And, as she says, word did get around. Pretty soon Kristen found herself in demand as a ski model. "That sounds a lot more glamorous than it is," she says. "Like most jobs, it's actually mostly hard work. You make two turns, then you hike back up the hill. Then you make two more turns and you hike back up the hill again. Do that 10 or 15 times and that can really wear you out."

Soon, she also had an offer to appear in a Warren Miller movie. "The weather out here is so nice," says Kristen. "There are a lot of good days for photography."

Once she achieved some visibility, she began to attract sponsors. "It was great," she says. "I found that in the winter, at least, I could make a living doing what I love."

But those were the winters. As the snow began to melt, Kristen headed for San Francisco, where, for the summer months she worked as a nurse in a pediatric ICU. "It was quite a change," she admits.

It turned out to be by far more of a challenge than anything else she'd ever done. "Day in and day out, I dealt with families going through what must be the most emotionally draining thing you can imagine, the illness and sometimes death of a child," she says. "The nurses I worked with were always asking me about my 'other life' and talking about how hard it must be. Believe me, what they do is way more difficult than being a professional athlete. I have tremendous respect for them."

Kristen led the double life of professional skier and nurse for 11 years. "Eventually, I had to leave San Francisco," she says. "Although I still continue to work part time to 'support the habit,' I was burned out at the PICU. I had to leave that part of nursing. I made the move to Tahoe full time."

Fortunately, by then Kristen was able to support herself year around by skiing. She began to travel more. "Now people have been basically everywhere," she says. "Travel, per se, is not as exotic as it was before. "So I try to do it differently. I've always had a curiosity about things, a quest for learning, a desire to challenge myself. You learn so much when you put yourself into another culture. Unless you've been to a third world country, you don't realize how many people's lives consist of just trying to get through the day."

One trip took her to Greece. "Few people consider that Greece is about 80 percent mountains," she says. "We stayed at the beach, but then we'd go up to the mountains to ski." Another trip took her on a trek through Burma and Nepal. Yet another time, she mountain biked in Bolivia at 17,000 feet. "That was a real adventure," she says. "It was pedal two strokes. Stop. Breathe. Pedal two strokes. Stop. Breathe." The opportunity to crew on a sailboat from Baja to Costa Rica was not as successful. "We were out in the middle of the ocean for days," she said. "I found out that was an adventure I didn't need."

A more recent trip took her to Kenya. "We had to climb eight days on animal tracks to ski the worst snow ever," she says. But still the trip had its lighter moments. "The porters couldn't believe that we would carry all this gear through the jungle. They were even more puzzled why anyone would climb up a mountain just to ski down it. I tried to explain about chair lifts and even showed them a post card I had that pictured one. They nodded politely and then asked, 'Well, why didn't you bring the chair with you?'"

She's found that true adventure traveling can be a humbling experience, as well. "You can be skiing in the mountains in Switzerland and think you're really on some tough terrain and along comes this little family. You realize that to them, skiing is just another form of transportation."

Closer to home, Kristen tried the World Extreme Championships in Alaska. "I always love to test myself," she says. "I knew I was a solid skier, but I'll admit I was never so scared in my life. Right at the start, one of the skiers fell through a cornice. In a competition like that, they don't want to bomb the snow, so they just roped off that area. But this guy had to go over and check it out. He broke through, tumbling over rocks on a 50-degree slope and was killed. Sure, I'd seen people hurt themselves, break a leg or an arm, but seeing this was really a profound thing. I have never looked at snow quite the same since."

Like most of her fellow athletes, the quest to better understand one sport got her involved in another. "Over the years, I'd come to realize just how big the mountains are and how intimidating they can be," she says. "I knew that if I were serious about moving up to the next level in skiing, I would need to know much more about the mountains themselves. I needed to really understand about glaciers and storms and avalanches."

The logical step was into mountaineering.

"Any book you read on mountaineering is full of harrowing stories left and right," she says. "Even the experts, the best people, die at this sport. Most people do sports under very controlled conditions. They ski on groomed, marked trails. If the weather is bad, they stay home. In a sport like mountaineering, you have to deal with many unknown factors at once. The weather can change in a matter of minutes. There is no telling how your body will react to the altitude. And most of the unknown factors will be entirely out of your control. From nursing I had learned that to preserve life you have to persevere and make it through. From rock climbing I'd learned that the more the effort, the greater the reward. There's nothing like putting yourself out there where you know it's all up to you."

Although when she climbs Denali, she will go with two other women, Lel Tone and Jessica Repp, in a way it will still be an individual challenge. "When you team up with people like you have to do in this sport, I would have to say that what you look for is the quality of people, not the quantity. Teamwork is very important, but it is also necessary to be cautiously confident in your own abilities. There should definitely be a leader in any group, but each person should know how to act self-sufficiently and be able to make both logical and group decisions."

"I look at climbing not as conquering the mountain, but more as being allowed to climb it, she says. "The mountain will tell you when this is possible. The mountains are very spiritual, sacred places on which we are sometimes fortunate enough to travel. You have to know your limits and respect what the mountain is telling you. Sure, we'd all like to say we made the summit, but we have to realize that maybe this won't be our time to do it. We know that no one was meant to live on these peaks. No summit is worth major injury or death. If we have to quit, we have to quit."

Not surprisingly, training to climb North America's tallest mountain is very serious business, even for women in superb physical shape.

"The more we can learn before we start, the better," says Kristen. "Because there are so many unknowns, you have to learn as much as you can about the things you can control.

Training is so much more than being fit. That's a mistake too many people make. It just amazes me to see people come out and start to climb a mountain when they don't even know how to put a pair of crampons on. You know they're in for a lot of trouble. You absolutely have to take the time to work out all the glitches. For example on Denali we know we're going to cross a glacier. It's only seven or eight miles total, but that's seven or eight miles at 12,000 or 13,000 feet. That makes all the difference. No matter how strong you are, you have to train hard for the effects of the altitude. Not only do you need to worry about altitude sickness, you have to be fully prepared for an immediate change in the weather, as well. One minute you're so hot you're down to one layer. Then along comes a cloud and you can't get warm fast enough. Then there are the winds that can blow upwards of 140 mph. You have to practice and practice to prepare for that."

Although the climb is still more than three months away and she still skis regularly, Kristen goes out on a trail and does two climbs a week on her skis. She also does a lot of Nordic skiing that stresses aerobic fitness. Recently she did an 18-mile Nordic race.

Diet is another important consideration for her. "In mountaineering, you always have to think about three things," says Kristen, "the cold, the altitude, and keeping yourself hydrated." Each presents a challenge, and sometimes meeting one need complicates meeting another. "When you're climbing at that altitude you burn from 2,000 to 4,000 calories a day. You should also drink at least four liters of liquid. Unfortunately, the altitude sometimes makes you nauseated and the weather can be so bad the last thing you want to do is worry about cooking. But you can't let either of those things get to you. If you get dehydrated or weak from lack of food, you won't be able to go on. No matter what you do, they say you'll lose at least five to ten pounds, so I'm trying to put on an extra 10 pounds before I go."

Although it would be possible to train alone, Kristen does not recommend it. "I find that training with friends tends to push me," she says. "I prefer to train with people who are better and more skilled. That way I have keeping up with them as a goal. They keep me motivated, and most of all, make it fun."

One such training exercise is a 24-hour mountain bike race she's now done twice. "I do this as part of a team of five," says Kristen. "There are four guys and I'm the token girl. It's really grueling. One time it snowed during the night ride. One year my lights went out at the very end and I crashed. But we placed 5th one year and 4th the next out of 250 teams in our group, so I guess we did OK."

Windsurfing is another sport she thinks helps prepare her both for mountaineering and skiing. "It reminds me a lot of skiing where you carve the board and pick a line to gain speed," she says. Although she learned to windsurf on Lake Michigan, she now does it mostly in the San Francisco Bay. "I like being able to sail in the 30 mph winds and do the waves on a short board," she says. "It takes the sport to the next level."

To prepare for the cold and for emergency situations, she's been practicing snow camping and building snow caves. "Because of the lower barometric pressure in the Arctic and the wind, it's one of the coldest climbs in the world," says Kristen. "The summit, at 20,320 feet, is actually the equivalent of a 22,000 Himalayan peak." The top of a mountain also has one of the most unpredictable climates anywhere, so practice means not just learning how to do things, but to do them quickly and efficiently and learning to do as much as possible with gloves on.

Not surprisingly, mountaineering is a gear intensive sport. To cope with weather that will range from balmy to well below zero, Kristen and the two other women will be both wearing and carrying an impressive amount of stuff. Like most cold weather athletes, they'll dress in layers. Next to the skin, they'll be wearing undergarments that wick moisture, rather than absorb it. Next, they'll wear pants or bibs and jackets made of Gor-Tex or other breathable, waterproof fabrics, along with socks, gaiters, boots, hats, balaclavas, gloves, mittens, goggles and sunglasses with a variety of lenses.

They'll carry a 40-pound pack and drag a 60-pound sled that will attach to the harness that will hold the ropes that will connect them to each other. In the pack and on the sled they'll have ice axes, carabiners, water bottles, extra boots, hiking poles, sleeping bags, ground pads, crampons, headlamps, eating and cooking utensils, a stove, repair kits for all this gear and all the food and personal toiletries they'll need. In case of emergency, they'll also have a CB radio they can use if they need to summon help from the ranger station. "We're also taking along compasses, altimeters and wind meters," she says. "Although I'm not sure I'll always want to know exactly what they say."

Since Kristen has a number of sponsors, most of her gear will be supplied to her. Thus, she'll have North Face clothing, Rossignol skis and Smith Sport optics. "It's great to have their support," says Kristen, "but I wouldn't do a thing like this if I didn't really believe in their products. Mountaineering is a sport where gear is key. It can save your life. Since I know they always have other athletes like me test their gear,

I'm confident that it will perform."

"I have to really hand it to those early explorers who did those big climbs in those heavy leather boots and clothing that was not even waterproof, much less wind resistant," she says. "Now at least everything is lighter and easier to carry."

Unlike a day hike that is pretty up the hill and back, an endurance climb like Denali involves a good deal of strategy. "A lot of it is about ferrying the load you're carrying and getting used to the altitude," says Kristen." Although the climb is treacherous and very demanding, it is at least marked and camps are situated at 12,000, 14,000 and 17,000 feet. "You carry with you what you'll need for 20 hours," she says. "You take your gear into the camp, mark it with your wands and go back and sleep at the next lower lever. At 14,000 feet, you rest for two days. Depending on how everyone feels, you go on. If one of us doesn't feel well, we'll go down another level. Mountain sickness is unpredictable and treatable only by descending. Then you just have to wait it out. It's not like some things where you can just gut it out and go on. If you do you'll be risking pulmonary or cerebral edema and both of them can be life threatening. I remember when I was in the Himalayas. I could feel my heart racing. That was really scary. A lot of people try to ignore it, but you shouldn't. It's just a fact that humans aren't designed to live that high. So you have to climb at a pace you can cope with.

"I guess that's one of the attractions of climbing with other women," says Kristen. "We're good friends and we communicate well with each other. I don't think with women that egos get in the way as much as with men. Guys are more likely to get bummed because they think someone else might beat them to the top. That's such a guy thing. That's what usually gets men in trouble. As long as you don't have summit fever, you'll do better. I think that's why women make good mountaineers. They're patient.

"Yet, you have to be really focused, too," she says. "Anyone who's ever competed in any sport understands the role psychology plays. If you aren't focused, you're finished before you start. You just have to remember that everyone has an off day. It may be a physical problem. It may be psychological. But if you're not there for some reason that day, it's bound to affect not only how well you do, but, maybe more importantly, whether you're enjoying yourself. It's the psychology that can put you to the next level."

"In mountaineering, I think you have to be focused with every step," says Kristen. "It's always a mental exercise. If it's really cold and snowing hard, you can't waste time and energy thinking about how miserable you are. You need to focus and mentally walk through what you're trying to do. You can't be moaning about the fact that there's no one to help you out. You have to set your sights on the next 500 feet or the next landmark. Then when you get there, you set another goal. I think it's as important to practice attitude as it is to practice skills.

"I also think you need to always focus on the positive. I like to see what I do as a series of successes. Those successes are what motivate me toward my goal," says Kristen. "I think that's what I like about mountaineering. It is very goal oriented. I like the fact that it takes a great degree of patience.

"You never know everything, but at this level of mountaineering, there is no room for self doubt, either," she says. "I wouldn't do any competition if I didn't think I could succeed. If you ever think you can't do it, you probably can't.

Instead, you have to start in your comfort zone and build upon that. If you lack confidence, you'll probably hurt yourself or fail. When I did the World Extreme Competition, I knew I could do it. It was a step up to the next level for me, but I was up for the challenge. Out of the 35 contestants, only six were women. I ended up fourth, but gained a tremendous amount of confidence. It was a real eye opener."

In May 2001, Kristen Lignell and Lel Tone climbed Denali, one of the most difficult mountaineering challenges in North America. They are pictured here at 16,000 feet.

Like many of her fellow female athletes, Kristen has found both skiing and mountaineering to still be male dominated sports. Like most other successful women athletes, however, she tries not to let that get in the way. "The important thing is to know your ability and know where you fit into the competition," says Kristen.

"Even so," she says, "It's frustrating that it's still a lot harder for a woman to get sponsorship in the more challenging sports. Men are still more respected and sought after. Even when you're at the top of your sport, the men in it always make more. It's very frustrating. So, especially at the beginning, it's hard to make a living at it. Sometimes I wonder if I shouldn't have considered taking up golf."

Gradually, however, she thinks the attitudes may be changing. "The last Olympics were another important milestone for women," she says. "The public saw strong, able women like Mia Hamm and the girls who play hockey getting a lot of the spotlight. Lynn Hill has also always been one of my role models," says Kristen. "She has a terrific following and has certainly shown that a woman can do even better than most men in a very tough and demanding sport."

Kristen also gives at least some credit to reality TV. "People just seem more interested in at least watching someone else test their limits.

"Each sport has its unique challenges and I guess that's what attracts me to them, as well," says Kristen. "I look at Sarah Fisher and what she does seems absolutely crazy to me. But I'm sure she must think the same about me. It's all in what you're trained to do. Once you're trained well, your sport becomes second nature to you. Then all you need is the self-confidence and experience. That's why I think many women excel more in their 30s and beyond. I know this woman in her 60s who lives in the mountains in Alaska. She just recently decided to try running a marathon. The only place she has to train is on the runway of the lodge her family operates, so every day she goes out and runs around and around that runway. When people have a goal, they'll do whatever it takes to get them there."

Kristen admits that at least part of her attitude has to do with where she lives. "Lake Tahoe is an athletic Mecca," she says. "So, I don't think it's at all unusual for people to always be out doing challenging sports. When I go back to Michigan, my family is always asking me why I can't just relax, why I'm always wanting to ski or ride my bike or do something outdoors.

"Sports are just a part of me now," she says. "They are a passion—what makes me feel alive. Sure there are sacrifices. When you compete at this level, you have to juggle your work and your personal life. You have to decide whether or not you'll have a family. Yet, I truly believe that everyone should be passionate about something, whether it's a sport, their family, a hobby, or their job. Having a goal helps us grow and thrive."

"Just this last weekend I went to a memorial service for two teenagers who died in an avalanche out here – just behind my house, actually. I coached one of those kids from age five to eight. It was a devastating thing for the families and this whole community. But at the same time it made me realize how precious every moment is and how fortunate I've been.

"When you're willing to challenge yourself, there's always something new and different to do and each experience lets you learn something more about yourself. I remember particularly going skiing in the mountains in Alaska. They fly you up to the top of a mountain and you realize that you may be the first person that ever skied that place. That's an incredible rush. Before I started down the slope I remember saying to myself, 'Who would ever have thought...'

"Those experiences are out there for everyone," she says. "All you have to do is go find them."

7

Go Fast or Go Home!

A Profile of Kim McKnight—Tesoro Arctic Man Ski and Sno-Go Classic Skier

Many extreme sports are highly individual, testing one skilled and daring athlete against another in a race where hundredths of a second count. An increasing number of extreme competitions, however, are now beginning to involve the combination of several skills, requiring not just individual expertise but carefully coordinated teamwork. Few competitions illustrate this concept better than the Tesoro Arctic Man Ski & Sno-Go Classic.

The Arctic Man promotes itself as "one of the world's toughest downhill ski races and an exciting snowmobile race, all in one." And it certainly must be. The event takes place in Summit Lake, Alaska which, according to founder and promoter Howard Thies, is basically out in the middle of nowhere. Everyone, participants and spectators alike, assemble at the site on Easter weekend and create an instant village of from 15,000 to 18,000 people, all camping out in tents or living in their RVs. For this one weekend a year, Summit Lake becomes Alaska's fifth largest city. A massive beer tent provides the center of activity for spectators, the media and the participants—eating together, partying together and trading stories about the day's events.

The day of the event, the skier and all her gear are hauled by a snowmobile up to a summit elevation of 5,800 feet. There are no cushy chairlifts or gondolas here. At a signal from an official, the skier tucks her arms tightly around her body and blasts off down the course, dropping 1,700 feet in less than two miles to a narrow canyon below. By the time she reaches the canyon, she is traveling somewhere between 70 and 85 mph.

In the canyon, her teammate waits, revving the engine of the snowmobile and holding the handle of a towrope similar to the ones used by water skiers.

As the skier appears behind her, the driver of the snowmobile quickly accelerates until she has matched the speed of the skier. At a designated point (and while they are still going 70 to 85 mph) the snowmobile driver holds out the handle of the rope. The skier grasps it, reeling in a section of the rope so she won't be jerked off her feet when the rope plays out to its full length behind the snowmobile.

The two then roar down the canyon through the bumps and ruts created by previous teams. At the end of the canyon there is another hill. The snowmobile tows the skier to the top of it. The two then separate with the snowmobile veering off to the right as the skier heads down the hill, dropping another 1,200 feet to the finish line and the wildly cheering, beer swilling crowd below. Course records are still held by the men's team of Peter Kakes and Johnny Martin, who achieved the fastest speed of 88.3 mph in the pull section and Eric Heil and Len Story who scored a time of 4:17:29.

Of the 40 teams that can participate, half of them are snowboard/snowmobile teams. So far only 10 of the teams are women. Another 10 are recreational teams who are not in contention for awards. Prizes include $60,000 in cash, a snowmobile and, perhaps ironically, considering the location of the *sport, four Alaska Airlines round trip tickets to warm, sunny Mexico.*

* * *

Like many little girls in the early 1980s, Kim McKnight was told that because she was a girl, she couldn't play hockey. Although this little girl was growing up in a family of brothers and was often more than a match for them, hockey in Revelstoke, British Columbia was a boy's sport. And that was that.

A setback like that might have caused other little girls to give up or to pursue more "acceptable" sports like gymnastics or horseback riding, but not Kim. So she couldn't play hockey. Well, then, there was always rock climbing, competitive swimming and soccer. She did those and did them well all through high school. But skiing was to emerge as her favorite.

"When you have three younger brothers, let's say there's a certain incentive to compete," says Kim. "Those guys always liked to race and it worked for all of us. There was no way I was going to let them beat me at it and they certainly didn't want to let their older sister get the best of them."

Being involved in outdoor sports was also a family thing. "My parents both grew up on farms," says Kim. "Being outdoors was always a part of their lives and they passed that on to us kids. Living in the mountains in Canada, most of the kids I grew up with liked to do outdoor things, too, so most of our social life was centered around things you could do outdoors."

Before long she was entering a lot of speed skiing competitions, including some World Cup events. "These were really challenging events," she says. "Around here we have some of the steepest and best runs in the world."

After completing her education, Kim moved to an even better place to ski, Whistler, BC. "This is just the most beautiful place," she says. "And the skiing is always fantastic."

At Whistler, like many competitors and most of her friends, Kim holds a day job at the resort, teaching skiing and waitressing on the side. "I really like teaching, especially the kids," she says. "Teaching complements what I do competitively. I think teaching is a real help since when you teach, you are emphasizing the basic skills over and over again. When you do that, you don't forget them. Teaching also allows me to be practicing all the time. Up here the season is so long, that even in the summer I usually get to ski some."

In the summer months, Kim also serves as a trail guide. "I have to do things that keep me outdoors and keep me active," she says.

There is certainly a lot to do around Whistler and being the adventurer she is, Kim was always on the lookout for another challenge. Soon, she heard a group of friends talking about something called the Arctic Man. Since it seemed to involve speed skiing and she was a pretty good speed skier, it seemed like just her kind of challenge. Some mutual friends got her in touch with Lisa Phillips, an expert snowmobiler, and they decided to give it a try.

"Lisa's only 19, a good deal younger than I am, but she has a lot of experience," says Kim. "Like me, she has several brothers and she grew up competing with them so I was pretty sure she had both the skill and the drive to do this. I think we've developed a good partnership."

Although both had confidence in their separate abilities, they didn't really know how they'd work together until they got to Alaska for the competition. "After we'd gone over the course a few times," says Kim, "we were pretty sure we could do it.

"It's not that it wasn't a challenge," says Kim. "The skiing part of the competition was not all that new for me. I knew pretty much what to expect. So at first all I could think about was the sled (snowmobile) and what Lisa would do. But in this competition you do better if you only focus on one thing at a time. I soon found out that you can't be thinking about what the sled is doing. You have to be confident that she will know what to do. Her job is to match your speed and then hold out the handle (of the towrope). Your job is to grab it. Then she stops thinking about you. Her job is to get ahead of you, find the best line (path through the canyon) and go as fast as she can."

"When you look at the tapes, it looks like there's constant pressure on the rope at all times," says Kim, "but that's not the case at all. In addition to just holding on at those speeds, because of the terrain you're constantly increasing and decreasing speed. When the sled goes around a corner, there's suddenly a slack in the rope. You have to be ready to take that up so you won't be jerked off your feet when she accelerates again. Believe me, you aren't just standing there and letting the sled pull you. Also, needless to say," she adds, "you have to keep your balance. If you catch an edge at 70 or 80 miles per hour you're in for a pretty big spill."

"At the top of the hill, there's a marker where the skier has to let go," says Kim. "At that point the sled veers off to the right and it's a real challenge for her not to go over the top. But, again, you can't be thinking about that. You can only think about what you need to do next. Sometimes you can get a little extra speed if the sled can whiplash you, but basically all you need to do is let go. That isn't very hard except for the fact that you're doing it when you're at your fastest speed."

Although Kim and Lisa thought they saw a few short cuts during practice, last year during competition they stuck to their original plan. "We figured we'd better go with the course we'd practiced," says Kim.

"Even though I'm still one of the few women who competes, I don't do it for that reason," says Kim. "In fact, one of my main concerns in entering was that there wouldn't be enough women to compete against. I wanted to do it because it was high risk. I'm always trying to encourage skilled women athletes to try this. I find it frustrating that they won't even give it a try. But, that hasn't stopped me. If other women don't want to try it, I'll go anyway."

Because Kim stays active in both skiing and other sports, she doesn't train specifically for the Arctic Man competition. "But, every day I do something," she says. "I think it's a lot more fun to train by mountain biking or wakeboarding or something else than doing something repetitive at the gym. The other thing I like about cross training is that doing other sports engages my mind, my whole body and my nervous system. No matter what sport you do, you need to learn to be in tune with your body. You need to know how your body works so you can anticipate what it will do. Plus, it's just a lot more fun to do other sports. It's good to push yourself to learn something new."

Kim has found that wakeboarding has been a tremendous help in preparing for the Arctic Man. "There are a lot of similarities in the sports," says Kim. "It's one thing to be able to ski fast and quite another to be towed around by a vehicle. It was also very helpful to practice grabbing the handle and dealing with the rope."

"I also compete all the time," she says. "So I don't have a chance to forget what it is like to get that adrenaline rush, either."

Unlike endurance sports like the Iditarod, the Indianapolis 500 or a triathlon, the Arctic Man is more like wakeboarding or skydiving—a very intense experience for a very short period of time. "Because of that, you have to eliminate as many of the variables as you can," says Kim. "Once you head down that hill you have to give that run your entire focus, you can't be worrying about whether you have on the right clothes or you put the right wax on your skis."

"In some ways, getting yourself ready for the Arctic Man is easier than it would be to train for an endurance sport," says Kim. Unlike Dee Dee Jonrowe or Kristen Lignell, she doesn't have to think about lugging, equipment, clothing and more than a week's food around. "But I'd say in many ways it's generally much more physically demanding. You finish the entire competition in less than five minutes. There is no time for a rest at any point. This is a very high impact sport and you put a tremendous amount of pressure on your legs 100% of the time."

By being active and physically fit, Kim doesn't find that she needs to follow a specific diet. "I don't do anything special," she says. "My parents are doctors and I grew up with competitors, so there was always an emphasis on good nutrition. I think the best diet is the one that provides the best nutrition. Everyone, athletes and non-athletes alike, should drink a lot of water and watch their fat intake. Beyond that, what you should and shouldn't eat is pretty much a gray area. But then, I ski every day, so I burn a lot of calories. Because of

that, I can treat myself to a junk food splurge once in awhile.
I had some coaches that were really strict about diets and
were always lecturing us about not eating desserts and so on.
But I've found that if I'm too strict I end up losing weight
because I burn so many calories.

"I do believe that when you eat is important, though," she
says. "You would never want to eat right before you compete,
but since a lot of events don't get started until noon, I always
try to have a good breakfast. My favorite is an egg sandwich
on whole wheat toast. That gives me the energy I need without filling me up too much."

Since the competition is held in the mountains in Alaska, weather, is, of course, a factor in the Arctic Man competition. "Because this race is so short, you have to be absolutely ready for whatever weather conditions you face," says Kim, "especially since they can change a lot even from the time you're at the bottom of the hill until you get to the top."

Even though Kim doesn't have to carry her clothing with her while she's competing, she still has to bring a variety of types of it with her to the race.

"Weather makes a huge difference," says Kim. "Learning to deal with what works best in what conditions is one of the challenges of this competition. Whatever the weather, Kim wears a tight rubber speed suit, a helmet and goggles. Her skis are very long and strong. "The bindings also need to be a lot beefier," says Kim. "While most recreational skiers might set their bindings at 5 or so, for this competition, I would set mine at about 20."

Although many competitors have fancy and extremely expensive custom-made helmets, Kim finds the "off the rack" ones sufficient. Good goggles, however, are very important. "You can only imagine what would happen if your goggles were to fog up on you," she says. She also carries along several different lenses ranging from dark gray or brown to yellow.

Wax is another important bit of gear to a skier of Kim's level of expertise. "It makes a big difference whether you're going to be skiing on fresh or old snow," she says. "It's also important what the temperature of the snow is. We always take the temperature of the snow before we put on the wax."

She's pretty much prepared for any type of weather. "Having grown up doing so many things outdoors has made a big difference in my ability to handle the weather," says Kim.

"I'm used to getting up and going out there no matter what it's like. At Whistler, I'll often go skiing in totally white-out conditions. My friends think I'm crazy to do that, but by now I know this mountain well enough to be able to know where I am all the time, so I can essentially feel my way down without having to see that far ahead.

Kim Knight is one of the few women who competes in the Tesoro Arctic Man Ski & Sno-Go Classic, an event in which the snowmobile and skier reach speeds in excess of 80 mph.

"It's always more intimidating to compete in bad weather," says Kim. "But you have to be fully prepared to race on any day. Everyone has to deal with the same weather. It's one of the things that makes the event so competitive."

To Kim, however, attitude is the main thing that separates the successful competitors from the unsuccessful ones. "It's so easy to beat yourself," she says. "That's another reason why I think coaching kids has been good for me. Kids tend to be very honest. They'll say exactly what they're thinking. And you can really see how their attitude affects their performance. If a kid is moaning and complaining about the fact that he's cold or his feet hurt or he doesn't feel like skiing that day, you can always see it in his performance. He's defeated before he starts. On the other hand, a kid who says, 'Wow, this looks like fun' will succeed even if she's less experienced or not as naturally athletic as the other kid. Mental attitude is a huge part of this.

"Obviously, to compete at this level you have to have the physical and technical skills, but I've found that the psychology of competing is equally important," says Kim. "Some people are excellent skiers, but they just don't compete well. In addition to not moaning about the hardships, you have to truly believe that what you're doing is fun. You have to also honestly believe that you are good. You can never let yourself say, maybe I can do this or maybe I might fall or maybe the weather will slow me down. You have to believe 100% in yourself."

Kim, like Lynn Hill, is also a great believer in visualization. "This event happens so fast that you have to be constantly focusing on what's up ahead," she says. "It's like when I go out on one of those white-out days in Whistler. I'm honestly confident that I can ski that run, even if I can't actually see two feet in front of my face. So the chances are that I will do it successfully. Doing the Arctic Man is the same. After I've practiced it for a few times, I can see it in my mind. When I get to each point in the run, it's easier to do it because the reality of the situation is just like I pictured it in my mind. If you ever start to doubt yourself, then you begin to make mistakes and that can get you injured."

Due to the nature of the event, Kim and the other competitors are literally surrounded by other people a lot of the time, but when they're competing they are totally focused. "Most of the fans are at the bottom of the course, but there are still a lot of people at the top," says Kim. "There are the other competitors, of course, and also the officials and people helping the competitors get ready. But, honestly, you don't really notice them. I describe that time right before the run as focused calm. You get yourself mentally prepared for the run, you visualize what you're going to be doing, you check out your gear one more time, then you're ready to go. If you're thinking about anything else, you've lost your focus and you're done.

"I won't say that I never notice the spectators, though," says Kim. "As you're coming to the end of the run and you see them all yelling and cheering, it really is a huge adrenaline rush. Then, when you're suddenly surrounded by them, it's great. Also, for the duration of the competition we live in the midst of them. They're parked all around you. It's a party atmosphere all the time. They're all involved in a sport they love, whether they're other competitors or just spectators. I find that I really feed off their energy.

"A lot of being able to focus just comes with experience," says Kim. "I've been competing for years so I know when and where to focus on myself and when I can relax and enjoy the stuff that's going on around me. By now, I'm used to having people watch me race, so a crowd isn't that much of a distraction.

"What motivates me generally is to be able to excel at something," says Kim. "I just love to ski. I feel lucky that I have the skill and had the good fortune to have grown up in a place where there were a lot of opportunities to test myself at a variety of things. It's just great to know that you're good at something. But, at the same time, I think it's always good to have a challenge to meet. Even though the men at the Arctic Man are physically stronger and bigger, I still find myself gauging my times against them. In fact, last year, I beat a few of them. I thought, All Right! When I ski, I usually go with the guys. I find that competing with them keeps me challenged. When you're at the top of your sport—when you can beat most of the women—you naturally find that you want to compete against the guys.

"Having said that," says Kim, "my personal philosophy is that winning or losing is not the issue. If that's all that matters to you, you can be easily defeated. What is important is that you achieve a goal that will make you happy. If I had won the Arctic Man, I would still know that I was behind some of the guys. Trying to beat them would become the next challenge for me."

Although she is intensely competitive, Kim feels that some people take competition to an extreme. "Some people are just too competitive," she says. "Winning is everything for them. They won't talk to the other competitors. Everything they do is a big secret. I'm not like that. If someone wants to know what kind of wax I'm using, I'll tell them. If someone broke a piece of equipment or needed to borrow my skis, I'd say, here, take them. Winning or losing doesn't make you better. Being challenged does.

"We have weekly races at Whistler," says Kim. "A lot of times I win, but not always. People say to me, 'Doesn't it make you mad when you lose?' My response is that if you win all the time, you don't learn anything. When I lose, I go back over what I did wrong and then try harder the next time to correct my mistakes. What gets you better is always trying to go to that next level.

"That's not to say there isn't some fear involved in this type of competition," says Kim. "This is a risky event and not to acknowledge that would be a mistake. Claiming to be fearless is just being arrogant and arrogance can get you in a lot of trouble. You have to acknowledge that there are risks. Then you find out what they are and do what you can to minimize them."

Although some athletes attribute good or poor performances to luck, Kim disagrees. "There's always a lot of talk about luck in competitions like this," she says. But usually if someone is injured or something goes wrong, luck didn't have anything to do with it. It was more likely lack of preparation or failure to work gradually up to what that person was trying to do. I would never just go out and practice full-out until I knew what I was up against. When Lisa and I practiced for the Arctic Man last year, we did half runs. We went through the course really slowly until we knew it. Then we could do it by intuition. We knew what to expect. If you want to get to a higher level in whatever you do, you have to build up to it."

While an injury could easily sideline Kim, being injured is not something she gives much thought to. "The key to competing at this level is to be in shape," she says. "And part of being in shape is to know how to keep yourself flexible so that if you fall, you aren't as likely to hurt yourself. Sometimes you hurt yourself anyway, like the time I broke my wrist—but could still ski—so I kept at it."

Once the Arctic Man is over, Kim thinks she may try the Spring Invitational or maybe the X Games or extreme speed skiing. "There's always more you can do," she says. "You can always go to a higher level. I just like to try new things. There is always something fun and challenging to do."

8

Catching the Perfect Wave

A Profile of Jodie Nelson—Surfer

The sport of surfing in the United States owes its initial popularity to an industry that has little to do with competitive athletics—the movies. Although surfing is believed to have originated in Hawaii where "he'e nalu" (wave sliding) existed well before the 1500s, there was little excitement about surfing on the continental US until Duke Kahanamoku, Tom Blake and Johnny Weismuller, all three 1920s screen idols, thrilled moviegoers with their muscular physiques and skills in the water.

As interest in the sport grew, so did the technology to support it. The original surfboards, that could weigh up to 150 pounds, were gradually replaced with lighter and lighter boards with sleeker profiles. The first Pacific Coast Surfboard Championships were held in California in 1928 and in 1930 Tom Blake received the first patent for a surfboard.

Perhaps inadvertently, the movie industry kept interest in surfing alive during the 1940s and 1950s through a series of films set in Hawaii staring Bing Crosby and Shirley Temple. In the 1960s, the sport received another boost, this time from the music industry as the songs of the Beach Boys and Jan and Dean gave even those shivering through a Midwestern winter visions of "hanging ten" in sunny southern California.

Although men had been competing in surfing since the late 1920s, in the late 1950s and early 1960s many women (some

*of whom provided the stunt sequences for the surfer movies)
began to compete seriously, as well. Linda Benson, for example, found time to win the Pacific Coast Women's
Championship in 1959, 1960 and 1961 while also doing the
action sequences for Gidget Goes Hawaiian. In 1975, Margo
Godfrey won the first all-women's international WISA Hang
Ten Championship at Malibu and became the first woman professional surfer.*

*During the 1970s, Jericho Poppler and Rell Sunn lobbied
hard to increase interest in women's professional surfing and
are largely credited for giving the sport the boost and attracting
the sponsors it needed to become the international competition
for women that it is today.*

*   *   *

Like many other California girls, Jodie Nelson grew up
quite literally on the beach. Her entire life has been spent
within a few yards of the breaking waves near Huntington
Beach. When her parents decided to move from California to
Colorado, she couldn't face giving up the ocean so she stayed
behind, renting from them the house she grew up in. "I can't
remember not being in the ocean. From the time I was an
infant I was always splashing around in it," says Jodie. "The
ocean is just a part of me. I can't imagine not being near it."

The family all loved the beach and water sports, but her
parents made sure she was also exposed to other options. "I
tried tennis, volleyball, soccer and gymnastics," she said. "I
was pretty good at some of them, but none of them ever
excited me much."

When she was 12, she got a job as a junior lifeguard. "At
last, I was back on the beach where I belonged," she says.
During that summer a friend suggested that she try a foam

board. "I kept working at it until I could stand up," says Jodie. "Once I got up the first time, that was it. I knew that's what I wanted to do. I wanted to be a surfer. It was the best feeling. I knew from that moment on that I would do whatever it took to get a surfboard. I worked hard, saved up my money and my dad took me to the shop to buy it. From that moment on, I just quit all other sports. Nothing about them interested me anymore."

Although her father had done some surfing in college, his skills were less than sharp, so Jodie hit the waves on her own. "No one taught me to surf," she says," and none of the rest of the family (she's the third of four children) even had any interest. But once I had the board, I went out in the ocean every day. I learned mostly by trial and error. I would watch what the other surfers were doing and try it until I mastered that particular skill, then I would try something else I saw them doing."

About the time Jodie was learning the basics, a neighbor boy also bought a board. "We had known each other all our lives and we pretty much learned to surf together," says Jodie. "Before long, we got pretty competitive. I think that helped a lot—being competitive in the sport as I was learning it."

Less than a year later, competition with the boy next door was no longer challenging enough. Jodie was ready to move up. Unfortunately, she couldn't find a way to do it.

It surprised me even then that there were so few other girls interested in the sport," says Jodie. "But I didn't let that stand in my way. If the girls didn't want to compete, I decided I'd just compete with the boys. Before long, I was in the top four and stayed there for a year. I have a feeling I upset a lot of egos doing that, but I was determined to get better and better and I felt that to do that I needed to be in competition."

"I also discovered that, even at that age, competition really made me happy," says Jodie. "I loved the challenge of it and the chance to make myself keep moving up to the next level. Since so few girls at school surfed, I played volleyball for a while, but, quite honestly, I just hated it. I only really did it to be social. What I always wanted to do was get it over with, go home and get in the ocean. It was the same with schoolwork. I was always a good student, but school wasn't what I wanted to be doing. It was something I made myself get through so I could get home and go surfing. Actually, that hasn't really changed. I still feel exactly the same way."

While still in middle school, Jodie competed in every local meet she could find. Soon, she was able to qualify for national teams. Like Sarah Fisher, Jodie spent a lot of her high school years traveling to competitions on weekends and in the summer. After her senior year, she began to dabble in the pro circuit and travel overseas. By the age of 20, she had won back-to-back victories in the West Coast Pro/Am Tour and in 1998 she qualified for the World Qualifying Series.

Like many extremely talented female athletes, she found the move from national to international competition a major adjustment. "I don't mean to sound braggy about this," says Jodie, "but when I was competing nationally as an amateur, I won just about everything. Except for Hawaii and Southern California, there really aren't many beaches in the US that generate the kind of waves that make for great surfing. The East coast shoreline and the Gulf of Mexico just aren't much good for this sport. So the number of American female competitors isn't that great. But in other parts of the world like Indonesia and Australia, the waves are awesome. I found out pretty fast that the girls who grew up there were really something."

The move from amateur to professional was another big step. "All of a sudden you're competing with women who have not only grown up where they got a lot of experience, but, being professionals, they've had the time to devote to the sport to be really, really good. Take the Australians," she says. "Basically the whole population of the country lives on the coast. With that many people growing up around water, there is just a much greater interest in and emphasis on the sport because there's so much more opportunity to do it. So the women have a lot more experience both with practicing and with competition.

"I was so used to winning that at first I had to really fight being depressed about losing," she says. "It was a real mental game for me. I just love this sport so much that for a while that was a real struggle."

That struggle led her to what has become a long-term association with a sports psychologist. "When you compete at this level," says Jodie, "there is no longer all that much difference between your skills and talent and the skills and talent of a lot of the people you compete against. Often the tiniest mistake can make the difference. So whether you win or you lose is quite often more of a mental game. It's as much about what goes on in your head as what is going on with your body. I found that I needed a mental trainer as much as a physical one.

"Obviously, professional competition is much, much harder," she says. "I've learned a tremendous amount since turning pro. You find that you approach competition in a much different way. But, despite that, I still enjoy it tons. I am really passionate about what I do and I couldn't be happier."

Despite Jodie's unbridled enthusiasm for the sport, she admits that her passion isn't always shared by fellow competitors. "I've seen a lot of cases where having to compete at this level has made people turn from loving the sport to hating it," she says. "For them, it just isn't fun anymore. It's work. It's a job and that's all it is to them anymore. Other people go the other direction and get just obsessed with it. It takes over their whole lives and they get carried away. I think if you're going to be successful, you have to love it and enjoy it, but you have to keep it in perspective." Her sports psychologist is helping her do that.

Like other professional athletes, Jodie has found that although she loves it, her sport is very much a business and it has to be treated as such. She is well aware that a sponsorship is not a gift or a grant with no strings attached. Currently that means that she must comply with the requests made of her by Huntington Surf & Sport, Pesce Surfboards, Arnette Eyewear, Reef Shoes, Blink Swimwear and Gravity Skateboards.

"The contracts you sign with sponsors are very specific about what responsibilities you have to them," says Jodie. "They're paying you to compete, but they are also paying you to represent their products. You are part of that company's marketing department." Like Sarah Fisher and Lisa Sher, that means that in addition to competing, Jodie must do photo shoots when the sponsor wants them done. She must also make public appearances, sign autographs and talk to fans.

"I take my responsibility to my sponsors very seriously," says Jodie. "I've seen some people take the sponsorship money and just lounge around. I guess sometimes they can get away with that, but I'm sorry, I think that's just wrong.

The sponsors are providing me the chance to do what I love. I owe them a return on their investment."

She's also aware that some sponsors choose to use spokespeople who don't compete. Instead, such athletes are used primarily as props for photo shoots. "That would certainly be easier, I guess," says Jodie. "I mean, they don't have to worry about bad weather or the schedules that competition imposes. They just wait for the best sunny day and go search out that perfect wave. That's kind of a niche thing," she says. "I think you'd have to really have a different attitude to do that."

For Jodie, in addition to appearances and photo shoots, sponsorship also means attention to what she does when she's off the clock. "I have a responsibility to carry a certain image," she says. "Sure, there are some sponsors out there that encourage their athletes to be reckless and do daredevil things, but I wouldn't do that. I know that the younger girls out there are looking at not just what I do in competition, but what kind of person I am. At that age, they're looking for role models and I think it's my job to be a positive one. I didn't have that growing up. Every once in a while there might be a small picture of a girl surfing in a guy's magazine, but that was all. Now athletes like me are in the spotlight a lot more. I think it's important that those of us who have made it to the pros do things that encourage these young girls—serving as an example of how to behave as a professional."

In return for the photo shoots and the personal appearances, Jodie gets a compensation package that includes several things. Like many other athletes, she receives a lot of free merchandise, and, in fact, as part of her contract is required to use and/or wear it. She also receives a salary and a travel budget. In her case, she is also eligible for a variety of incentives.

"It's kind of complicated," says Jodie, "but essentially incentives are given for performance and publicity. You get so much extra depending on how you rank in the standings at the end of the season. Then you also get incentives for getting magazine placement and placing well in readership polls and on videos."

Because figuring all of that out can be quite time consuming, Jodie has hired a professional manager. "I managed myself for awhile," she says. "But eventually all of that negotiating and paperwork just took too much time away from what I felt my primary responsibilities were. I let her do all that for me now. It's a much better situation"

In addition to competition and promotions, Jodie must still devote a considerable amount of time to training. "To compete in this sport, you must be in very good shape," says Jodie. "You have to take extremely good care of your body. Professional competition is a business. And I am the product."

Being the product is incredibly physically demanding. Unlike other sports, surfing requires little gear. The place where she competes, the ocean, is vast, unpredictable and relentless. Getting out to the waves requires tremendous upper body strength. Pulling one's body up out of the water onto the board requires not just agility, but a huge amount of power. Remaining balanced on the board requires, according to Jodie, "just about every muscle in your body." And more times than not, tons of water come crashing down on the top of the surfer at some point, plunging her several feet underwater in the midst of tides and undertows, requiring immense effort to get to the surface and retrieve the board.

Once on the surface, wave after wave can come rolling over your body. "You have to always be aware of where you are," says Jodie. "You can never turn your back on Mother Nature. If you do, you'll get worked every time."

Even in the same location, the waves are different every day. "Some days you're looking at huge waves and deep water," she says. "Then the next day you may be facing small waves and shallow water."

Depending on where the competition is, the sea floor may present life-threatening hazards. "Just the smallest mistake can be fatal," says Jodie. "I've seen people come up with pieces of reef stuck in their heads. I've seen people hit very hard by a heavy board."

In addition, surfing requires tremendous stamina. "You're always moving," says Jodie. "You're always fighting the water. It's very intense. Usually two to three heats a day will completely exhaust you, but if the competition calls for four or five, you have to somehow come up with the strength to do them."

She practices surfing a good portion of every day and follows a strict training regimen. "There isn't one right way to train for this sport," she says. "Even though women may be at essentially the same level of competition, each is still an individual whose body has individual needs. Also, as you get older and more experienced, your body is always changing. Your training regimen will change from time to time, too. I find that I do different things each year. I've tried yoga, swimming, running and working out at the gym. I also make regular visits to a chiropractor and a massage therapist."

Recently Jodie has switched to a different type of workout. "This was so strange at first," she says. "I was used to these gyms that were packed with all these machines. When I first walked into this place, I thought I must be in the wrong building. There was just nothing there. I couldn't imagine what I could get out of a workout that didn't involve weights and machines. I found out pretty quickly. It was so intense I couldn't walk for the next three days."

The regimen she now follows involves exercise balls, stretching bands and wobble boards. She's found that this kind of exercise is excellent for both strength training and balance. "At first I couldn't even stand up on the board," she says. "But now that I've got it, I think it's done a lot for me."

The bands her trainer works her out with both strengthen the muscles and provide a good stretch. "One of the bands connects to the floor," says Jodie. "You put it over your shoulders and do squats. It's like lifting 200 pounds." Jodie works out three days a week. "I always get in the water at least once a day, usually more," she says. "I also swim and run for cardio exercise."

An additional advantage to bands and balls is that they are, for the most part, portable. Since Jodie travels so much, she can generally take all the equipment she needs right along with her. When she can't, she just spends more time in the water. "When you surf six or seven hours a day, you get plenty of exercise," she says.

In addition to building strength and flexibility, unlike athletes who compete on the ground, Jodie must practice overcoming a potentially dangerous environment. She must know how to remain calm when a wave forces her under water for a prolonged period of time. Jodie practices this in a pool. "I get in and swim at least two laps underwater," she says. "It is important to be able to build lung capacity, but it is even more important to learn how not to freak out every time you can't immediately get to the surface. You have to get so you can remain calm, knowing that you can hold your breath until you get back up."

As far as diet goes, Jodie has found that a high protein, low carbohydrate diet works best for her. "I think of all the types of diets, this gives me the most energy," she says.

Like other athletes who compete in extreme weather conditions, Jodie never knows what she may be up against during competition. The waves she will ride on any given day have been created by storms and tides that have traveled thousands of miles. While race officials have some discretion in delaying a competition, often when the crowd has gathered and the sponsors have shelled out the money, the show must go on even if the conditions aren't ideal.

"You must always be prepared to compete in the very worst conditions," says Jodie. To prepare for the very worst, like many of the other women, she finds that visualization is invaluable. "Visualization is a big part of being mentally prepared," she says. "When you know things are going to be pretty difficult, you go over everything in your mind first. You visualize the walk to the beach, getting into the water, getting

*For Jodie Nelson, surfing is a full-time occupation that
requires intense physical and mental preparation.*

out to the wave, getting up on the board – the whole experience. Because you can't always rehearse it in reality, you
rehearse it in your mind. Then, when you have to do it,
you're ready for it. You always prepare for the worst," she
adds. Then, when it's easier than you thought, it's always a
pleasant surprise."

Sometimes the weather is not the only problem, however,

"One time I was in this competition in Santa Cruz," says Jodie. "For this particular event we were required to jump off this cliff into the ocean. I was a little late and got there after most of the other girls had already jumped. I rushed up to the edge and here's this huge sea lion just looking up at me. It freaked me out. I couldn't do anything until he took his sweet time getting out of the way."

Although she finds these unexpected situations to be frustrating, at the same time the unexpected is often what makes every competition unique. "Everyone is up against the same things," she says. "They have the same challenges to face that you do."

While a triathlon or a skydiving meet can be held almost anywhere in the world, there are really very few venues that meet all the requirements for a viable surfing competition. Competition at the professional level is, after all, a business. Because surfing is a sport with fairly regional interest in the US, it doesn't attract the large television audiences that sports like basketball or baseball do, so revenues may depend primarily on attendance. Jodie and the other women who compete are hoping that the increase in the numbers of television channels will someday mean that meets can be staged in more remote areas like Indonesia where the conditions are ideal.

But for now most competitions are held where there are a lot of fans. "In this country, that pretty much means Southern California and Hawaii," says Jodie. "And, realistically, Hawaii is really the market for surfing. It's different than anyplace on earth. There is a nine-mile coast with 50 different surf breaks, so there's a lot to choose from. In the winter, especially, they have these really huge swells. The waves are very powerful. It's a wonderful place.

"Hawaii is probably the world Mecca of surfing," says Jodie. Not surprisingly, many of the competitions are held there. "It's quite a scene," she says. "The whole length of the beach will be completely infested with people, some of them professionals, some amateurs, most just fans out to see what's going on. Sometimes you'll be out on the water and look in at the beach and there'll be 100 photographers with long lenses all pointed directly at you."

Once the crowd has gathered, unless the conditions are just truly unacceptable, the competition usually proceeds on schedule. "Unless you've done some serious surfing, it's pretty hard to understand what is and is not a good day to surf," says Jodie. "The huge waves are certainly the most dramatic, but sometimes the smaller ones can be the most challenging, especially if they're breaking over a reef or some other shallow water."

Unlike auto racing or the Arctic Man, where the fastest competitor always wins, surfing, according to Jodie, is very subjective. "There are all kinds of variables," she says. "Basically you're judged on how well you control a powerful turn in the best wave. Generally, you have about 20 minutes to make 10 attempts and the best three are counted."

It is not, of course, as easy as that. "It's entirely up to the surfer to choose the wave," says Jodie. "The biggest wave is not always the best wave. A big wave may close out on you. Also, waves do what they do with no concern about you at all. It's all about you being in exactly the right place at the right time. Then, even if you think you've done everything perfectly, one of the judges may just not like your style or the way you look or something. I guess I would compare it to figure skating in that regard."

Jodie has found that that's just part of being a seasoned professional. "If you can, you always watch all the heats that go before yours and see what the judges are rewarding. There's usually a pattern to what they do." Although some of the moves that result in good scores are traditional, Jodie has seen a change in the last few years. "I'd say the judges are beginning to reward much more aggressive moves," she says.

Unlike the extremely geary sports like dogsled racing, mountaineering and auto racing, surfing is a fairly straight-forward sport. Other than protective clothing like wetsuits, there's basically only one piece of equipment—the surfboard —and they're all designed about the same. They are all made of the same basic material—a foam core to give them buoy-ancy, a wood stabilizer in the middle and a fiberglass shell. Unlike skis, that are flexible, surfboards are rigid and range in length from five feet to almost nine feet in length.

The boards Jodie rides range from 5'8" to 8'4." Jodie finds that she uses all of them at one time or another just as Kim McKnight and Lel Tone wear different skis for different snow conditions. The big boards, known as "guns" are used when the waves are large and powerful and give the surfer more stability. The little boards, known as "fishes" are used for smaller waves. "The rest are used for everything in between," says Jodie. "I guess you could compare them to golf clubs. You use the one that's designed specifically for that situa-tion."

To catch a wave, the surfer lies on the board and paddles out. At the right moment she hoists herself up on the board and positions her feet on it. There are no straps or bindings on a surfboard like there are on waterskis, wakeboards or snowboards although, according to Jodie, some variations are now being developed. "Some people are getting into boards where their feet are strapped in so they can be towed behind a WaveRunner," says Jodie. "I've only done it once, just fooling around. It was pretty crazy."

Like most of her sister athletes, Jodie has made many sacrifices to stay at the top of her sport. "I'm constantly on the road," she says. "Sometimes I hardly have time to breathe before I have to go out and do something else. Sure I have days when I don't want to go to the gym. And there are days when the waves are pretty disappointing. When I got back from Australia where the waves were big and beautiful, the waves here in California were bad and dirty and it was cold. It may have been a little depressing, but I got right out there anyway.

"I guess you could say that surfing has taken over my life, but in a good way. I can't imagine what could be wrong with spending most of your time pursuing the thing you love most. It's taken me all around the world and let me meet really interesting people while I work at getting better and better.

"I love it so much," she says. "I love it more than anything. It's what drives me. What makes me complete. I love being a professional athlete. It isn't easy to compete at this level, but I know that, at the most, I may only be able to do this for a fraction of my life. And while I'm still able to do it, there are always other women out there who are also training very hard. I want to be the best. I will do what it takes to be the best. I know that, ultimately, that just means that I have to want it more than they do."

9

Trying to Fly

A Profile of Erika Sanborn—Skydiver

Although there is no way to tell for sure how birds feel about people, it is most definitely true that since the beginning of time, people have wanted to feel like birds. Chinese paintings many thousands of years old picture adventurers jumping from cliffs and towers, hopefully clutching umbrellas. One of Leonardo Da Vinci's most famous drawings is of a group of his fellow citizens soaring aloft in pointy-topped parachutes. As early as the 1780s, French balloonist Jean Pierre Blanchard created a silk canopy parachute. Unfortunately he broke both his legs in an attempt to illustrate how it worked. Andre Jacques Garnerin turned parachuting into a profession in the late 1700s, traveling around France doing skydiving demonstrations from hot air balloons.

The first woman recorded to have tired parachuting was Genevieve LaBrosse, Garnerin's wife, who floated safely down from a hot air balloon in 1798.

It wasn't until the invention of the airplane in the early 1900s, that what we now think of parachuting was born. The first successful jump from a plane was made by Captain Albert Berry in 1912. In 1919, Leslie Irvin made the first free fall jump using a hand operated parachute and is credited with creating parachuting as a sport.

Although thousands of soldiers became parachutists—either

willingly or unwillingly—during WWII, the sport didn't really catch on until the 1950s, involving, not surprisingly, many of the same soldiers who had learned the basics in the armed services. Most of the jumps these men made relied on surplus military supplies. Soon, even those who had no military experience were taking up the sport and skydiving clubs were formed around the world.

As interest in the sport grew, parachutists sought more and different gear. The saucer shaped white or khaki colored parachutes that were used by the military were soon replaced by the brightly colored and far more versatile rectangular parachutes made of ever-lighter man-made fabrics. To the relief of friends and families waiting on the ground, automatic activation devices and altitude sensors added a dimension of safety to the sport, as did an increase in the quality of skydiving instruction.

Yet, as all who try it will tell you, it's still a thrill every time.

* * *

Two young teenage boys sit side by side, strapped into the makeshift seats of the Cessna 182. Both watch wide-eyed as, at 9,000 feet, the door to the plane opens and the woman in the purple jumpsuit blows a kiss to the boys, and gracefully steps out into thin air. One of the boys stares in wide-eyed amazement at what he has just witnessed. Once back on the ground he tells everyone who will listen, "Man, you should have seen it, she just opened that door and jumped!"

The other boy just shrugs his shoulders. It's not that he isn't amazed every time he sees her do it, but by now he's pretty much used to it. The mothers of most of his friends play golf or run or sail. His mom jumps out of airplanes.

The boy is Kyle Sanborn and his mother, Erika, does

indeed take every opportunity she can to spread her arms and fly.

By her own admission, Erika, who grew up with four brothers, was always "the consummate tomboy." She swam in grade school and ran track in high school, but not competitively. "Mostly I just wanted to belong somewhere," she says. When a flyer posted in her college dorm announced the formation of a skydiving club she wanted to give it a try. "But when I asked my parents for the $50 it would cost for the first jump, they told me I was out of my mind. That was the end of that."

It wasn't until 1997 that she was finally able to give the sport a try. That jump literally changed her life.

In January 1988, although Erika had been a straight A student slated to be valedictorian of her college class and had already been accepted into graduate school, a rebound romance led to a pregnancy and a hurry-up marriage. Being the mother of two children (daughter Taylor was born in 1993) was a source of tremendous joy, but being married to the wrong man soon led to serious clinical depression. Although her husband and his family felt that her place was in the home, in 1995 he grudgingly agreed to allow her to take a part time job. A stint as a secretary in a physical therapy department of a local hospital led to a job as a CPR instructor. When a position as a Healthy LifeSteps educator became available, she was offered the job contingent upon finishing her degree. She graduated magna cum laude.

Having now regained at least a bit of the self confidence she had lost during the previous ten years, Erika eagerly agreed when a female friend suggested that they try skydiving. Predictably, her husband said no. "That was the beginning of my love for skydiving and my decision to live life for myself instead of everyone else," she says.

It was a courageous step. "I still hold the record for being the only woman ever to show up at our drop zone alone for a class," says Erika. "Usually boyfriends or husbands talk girl-friends or wives into jumping with them. Women almost never decide on their own.

"I made my first jump on August 9, 1997," she says. "That one was to prove I could. I made the second jump just two hours later because I loved the first one so much. I loved being my own person and I loved feeling free. I loved seeing my son watch me land and run up and say, 'Wow! You really jumped.' I loved everything about it. Jumping from that air-plane saved my life and allowed me to leave a very unhappy marriage."

Erika filed for divorce in January 1998, but it was not finalized until May 2000. "I figured there was just no way I could fight it out in court for my children, feed my family, pay child care expenses and pay an attorney for what turned out to be three years on the $7.25 per hour I was making working part time," says Erika. "So, although I loved it, I told my new skydiving friends I would have to quit."

Her drop zone owner would have none of it. Knowing that Erika had a lot of computer knowledge, he agreed to trade out the creation of a data base for free skydives. He even paid her a little extra and advanced her the money for gear. During those three tumultuous years, she continued to train, becom-ing a jumpmaster then an instructor, soon trading teaching for skydiving.

At the same time, although she had no experience in sales or senior living, Erika accepted a job as the marketing director of a local assisted living facility. "They said they were looking for someone who could take chances. What better way was there to prove that I could do that than jumping from perfectly good airplanes," she says.

Erika describes herself as a very competitive person, however, she says, "My life over the last three years has not been conducive to competition. Plus, sometimes I am my own worst enemy and am very hard on myself. I've needed this time to build my self-esteem and didn't think I should push myself too hard in areas where I was not sure of success."

She says that deep down, she thinks that someday she really would like to do something in the sport like participate in an all-girl 100 way or something equally amazing, for now she feels good about teaching and improving her skills.

"I enjoy teaching everyone," she says. "I am the only female instructor at the drop zone, so often other instructors will call me over to help with their female students. Sometimes I'm able to put students more at ease when they see that I not only did it once, but went on to become an instructor myself."

She has found somewhat to her surprise that women often do better at the sport than "big burly guys," although she finds that being a woman instructor works pretty well with the guys. "I had one man say to me, 'I'm scared to death but there is no way I'm gonna chicken out in front of a girl.'

"My favorite students are the unusual ones and ones that present a real challenge," says Erika. "They are often hard work, demanding and frustrating but in the end they enjoy it more and I'm rewarded more for having had the experience." Some of her more unusual students have included a 72-year-old nun and a 40-year-old man with MS in a wheelchair.

There's also the occasional person who has never been in a plane and who is afraid of heights. "I understand trying to overcome fear," she says, "but come on!"

She also does demonstration jumps for local clubs and organizations to help promote fund raising endeavors. "This is not exactly competing," she says, "but it is a competition with myself to see if I can give them a great show."

Because she has chosen not to compete, unlike DeeDee Jonrowe who purposely maintains a certain distance from her fellow competitors, Erika considers her skydiving buddies some of her best friends. "I don't put a lot of pressure on my self. I know that if I mess up, no one will be upset. But when I go to other drop zones or skydiving boogies, I always feel some extra pressure to perform. I haven't found a good way to handle that, but I'm working on it.

"What works best for me is to breathe deeply and when thoughts of failure begin to creep into my head I try to block them out by visualizing the skydive going perfectly. I deal with the trip to altitude by closing my eyes and doing breathing exercises. If I can't relax that way, I give myself something to do like a visual gear check of everyone in the plane. Little do they know I'm not neurotic about checking their gear. I'm neurotic about being stuck in the plane."

As in most extreme sports, there is not just one way to do it. "Skydiving includes many disciplines and each discipline has its extreme nature," says Erika. All have their risks. "Many think skydiving is extreme because the failure of the equipment would likely result in death," says Erika. "I find it extreme because there is no other sport that allows the freedom, the beauty and the discipline of free fall."

The discipline Erika participates in is called "relative

work." Other skydivers enjoy variations called head down, free flying, sit flying, tube flying and sky surfing. There are also variations in relative work like swooping, which involves seeing how far the skydiver can glide from one to five feet above the ground before landing.

Erika Sanborn, joins hands with other skydivers, free-falling at 120 mph.

"Head down is extremely high speed and is exactly what it sounds like," says Erika. "Rather than flying in the stable belly-to-earth position, people fly head down reaching speeds of up to 160 mph or even higher. Lots of camera flyers have gotten into this and it makes for very interesting photographs.

"Free flying and sit flying are like ballet in the air," she says. "They are really beautiful. Sky surfers are free flyers who jump with a board attached to their feet. It's like surfing in the sky. Tube flyers are free flyers who jump with huge cloth tubes. I haven't figured out the allure of that yet. At some point I hope to try it all, except for maybe that tube thing.

"Relative work is skydiving relative to other skydivers in the air and completing formations with those skydivers," says Erika. "Flying relative to others really feels like flying. It requires trust, discipline and awareness to maintain safety for yourself and for others. In the free fall stage of relative work, in the belly-to-earth position, we're falling at 120 miles per hour. There is nothing like it.

"Skydiving used to be only for thrill-seeking daredevils—mostly young men," says Erika. "Now with improvements in the equipment and more knowledge of the sport, many people who would never have tried something like this are giving it a try.

"Still," she admits, "skydiving mostly attracts those who want to 'push the envelope.' You can never fully appreciate it until you do it yourself. Some skydivers feel nervous and anxious before every skydive. An instructor once told me that if you aren't a little afraid, there's something wrong with you. Well, call me crazy, but I'm never afraid of the skydive and I'm always afraid of the plane ride.

"I love being outside the plane and I hate being cramped inside it," she says. "For the same reason I can't wear a helmet, I hate being shoved in a plane like a sardine. I am an intelligent person and I know how dumb that sounds but fear and phobias are strange things to explain. Also, my experiences as an instructor versus just another jumper on board vary tremendously."

Even though she admits that skydiving doesn't require the extreme physical fitness that many other sports do, Erika thinks it is important to stay in shape. Typically, she does an hour of aerobics and weight training seven days a week. She also watches her diet and refuses to train with people who are smoking.

"I believe that proper nutrition and healthy habits in general lead to better, more capable and more energetic skydivers," she says. "My common sense tells me so, but I have little to back that up. Some of the most unhealthy people I know are awesome skydivers."

Not surprisingly, skydiving takes a lot of practice. Some of the training (called dirt diving) is done on the ground. Skydivers also practice visualization. "Because skydives are comprised of a combination of maneuvers that are done in different combinations from dive to dive, the only real training for a skydive is more skydives," says Erika.

In addition to practice, skydiving also requires a good deal of knowledge of the physics of the sport. "In the first jump class, students are taught how to get into the correct body position, about forward glide of the canopies, how to turn, how to flare for a soft landing and land into the wind," says Erika. "Once students get past these basics and are into free fall, they have to learn how changes in their body positions cause them to fall faster, slower, more forward, backward, sideways, turn a full 360 degrees and, perhaps most importantly, how to stop."

When teaching others, Erika starts by drawing diagrams and lying on the ground to illustrate the various positions a skydiver must assume. "This is a sport that, by its very nature, encourages mentoring," says Erika. "It is also a sport from which you can never stop learning. I learn every time I get in the air whether I'm teaching a student or jumping with a friend. The physics of it all can only be learned by practice."

The pilots who take the skydivers up must also be specially trained and commercially rated. "New pilots fly first with an experienced skydiving pilot," says Erika. "It requires a special talent to be able to fly a fully loaded airplane, fly with the door open and maneuver the plane to close the door after the jumpers leave, fly over a spot and watch for skydivers and parachutes in the air. Some pilots are very intimidated by it. Those who enjoy it tend to stick around and usually end up jumping themselves. It looks like more fun to jump than to fly, so they have to give it a try."

The pilot Erika usually goes up with is another mother with a full time job. "Typically, people fly skydivers on the side in order to gain air time necessary for other licenses," says Erika, noting, however, that her pilot has recently also been bitten by the skydiving bug. "She has about 40 jumps now."

While many sports require very specialized gear, in no sport, even auto racing, is the right kind of gear more important to the safety of the participant.

"My children are my life," says Erika, "and all of the back-up devices on my gear are so they will never have to watch me plummet to earth without a parachute over my head. I am as careful as I can possibly be and still participate in a sport I love."

All skydivers wear a jumpsuit of some kind. Each suit is custom made for the jumper and how the suit fits can greatly affect the skydiver's performance. "A tight jumpsuit is worn by small people or people who for one reason or another don't fall as quickly as other skydivers," says Erika. "A loose jumpsuit is worn for the opposite reason and catches more air to slow you down."

Erika wears a tight, spandex and nylon jumpsuit called a Pit Special composed of "fun fabric" Erika sent to the manufacturer. Daughter Taylor picked out the colors. The suit has foam inserts sewn into the arms and legs as well as an assortment of pockets and zippers. Although students are required to wear helmets, Erika opts not to. "I'm claustrophobic and am more comfortable and free without it," she says.

While it is possible to buy a type of "footie" to go with the jumpsuit, "believe it or not, many skydivers jump barefooted or in Teva sandals," says Erika. "It's part of the free feeling. The breeze on your toes is another perk to the skydive."

All skydivers also wear an altimeter. "The altimeter is set to zero on the ground and counts down from the exit point so that you can maintain awareness of your altitude and deploy your parachute at the proper altitude," says Erika. "This is typically at around 2,500 or 3,000 feet for experienced skydivers."

Obviously, the most important piece of gear for a skydiver is the parachute rig. Most rigs today are a far cry from the bulky military surplus parachutes worn by the first amateur skydivers in the early 1950s. "Even in the three years I've been skydiving, the gear has changed by leaps and bounds," says Erika. "Containers are getting sleeker, more comfortable to wear and more durable. Modern parachutes are rectangular and act like an inflated wing. We fly and land them much like a pilot flies and lands an airplane. The fabric from which the parachutes are made and the slight variances in shape of the canopies are being modified and improved constantly. New parachutes are designed for better performance faster than skydivers can keep up with the changes.

Erika Sanborn's specialty is "relative work"—
where skydivers perform as a group and create intricate formations.

"The new designs allow skydivers to jump much smaller canopies than ever before. They are much more responsive and fun to jump, but the smaller they are, the less forgiving they are."

Like most students, Erika started jumping a 300-square-foot Falcon canopy that she describes as "fun, but very docile." From that she went to a 200-square-foot Maveric which was a little more responsive. "Then I got my first Zero P canopy, a fabric that is made to cut through the air more sharply and be a higher performance parachute," she says. "It was a Monarch 175, still pretty big, but my first 15 jumps on it scared me to death!"

Gradually, she moved to smaller and smaller canopies. "The more you jump the smaller you want to go," she says. She now jumps a Saphire 129. "It is very fun and very responsive and I have a healthy respect for its forgiveness and I don't do anything stupid under it," she says, commenting wistfully that someone who weighs a good 50 pounds more than she does jumps an Alpha 97.

The canopy is just one part of the parachute gear, however. Also included are all sorts of devices designed to make sure the parachute opens when it should. There are reserve pins and pilot chutes and main pins, cutaway handles and reserve static lines. Like most skydivers today, Erika also wears a Cypres, a computer that is designed to fire a small charge that cuts the closing loop and deploys the reserve parachute at a preset altitude if she has not deployed either her main parachute or her reserve chute.

Another consideration for skydivers is the wide range of temperatures they experience even on the balmiest of days. "In the dead of summer we wear next to nothing on the ground," says Erika. "Packing a parachute is hard work and you work up a sweat doing it. It can also be very warm in the airplane for the first few hundred feet. During cold weather jumping, skydivers find that they need to wear several layers. "It's about 30 degrees colder at altitude than on the ground, so if it's cold before you take off, it isn't a fun ride to altitude. Most people wear long underwear or thin insulating type fabric of some kind under their jumpsuit. Stocking caps, often with a full facemask and a helmet, if you wear one, and gloves are critical. It's important to maintain feeling in your fingers so that you can feel to deploy your parachute."

There is little sponsorship money in skydiving, so buying all this gear is usually up to the skydiver. "The only skydiving teams I know of that get their gear provided are the military teams," says Erika. "Even the skydivers you see on world record attempts have to buy specially made jumpsuits for the attempts at their own cost."

Jumpsuits cost around $180, other gear (even if you buy some of it used) can add up to around $2,500. The first jump course for a novice runs about $165 and subsequent jumps around $12-$17 each. Even the most ardent competitors pay all their own expenses to meets.

Although there is money to be won at some competitions, "You can't get rich jumping from airplanes," says Erika. "You don't get anything but satisfaction and recognition within the sport for records you set. Some people find this discouraging. I find it to be a part of what I like about the sport. It keeps people from participating for the wrong reasons."

Erika's role as an assisted living community executive director and her responsibilities as the mother of two children means that she's on call to someone virtually 24 hours a day.

Because she and her ex-husband have joint custody, generally she can be at the drop zone on the weekends. When the kids are with her, "We compromise," says Erika. "Sometimes they want to go to the drop zone with me, sometimes not. During the school year, I rarely skydive during the week because I need to spend my evenings helping with homework. After a stressful day at work, sometimes I would really rather forget about being responsible and go jump out of an airplane, but my kids always come first," she says.

She also carries a pager with her at all times, should an emergency arise at work "Fortunately, I have a fabulous staff and they are very capable of handling most things when I'm away, so there's usually not much of a problem." As for the residents of her assisted living facility, "They tend to treat me like a grandchild," says Erika, "and fear for my safety." To help overcome this obstacle, Erika invited them to witness one of her recent skydives and brought her parachute into the office and invited them to watch her pack it. One of her residents is also one of the original UDTs (predecessor of the Navy SEALs). "He likes to go out to the drop zone once in awhile just to visit with the guys and tell stories about what the old parachutes were like.

"There's no doubt that I am a better parent now that I have found a sport and a job that make me happy and give me something to look forward to," says Erika. "I've taken all the extra steps that most parents my age don't even think of, like making out a will, giving a friend power of attorney and setting up guardians for my kids if something should happen to their father and me. I think my kids will be better off having had the mom I am today for a short time if something tragic should happen than the mom I was three years ago for their entire lives.

"In skydiving, I'm inspired by every person who has the courage to conquer a fear or to go one step beyond what they thought they were capable of," says Erika. "People and human nature inspire and motivate me. I used to think the world was full of bad people because I have had a lot of bad people in my life. The people involved in the sport of skydiving have shown me that the world is full of good people who are not out to take advantage of others, but to help out and share something they love. I only know some of the people I jump with by their first names or their nicknames, but I would trust them with my life. There is a camaraderie among skydivers like nothing else I have ever experienced."

10

Straight Downhill: Over The Rocks and The Roots and The Bumps

A Profile of Lisa Sher—Mountain Biker

The sport of mountain biking, like surfing, had its origins in the US in California.

In the late 1960s, Gary Fisher, a bicycle racer, and his partner Charles Kelly, a roadie for the rock group Sons of Champlin, moved to Marin County. There, with Joe Breeze and Tom Ritchey, they organized a series of races for their favorite bikes: the heavy "cruiser" models of the time, known as "clunkers."

They weren't, of course, the first people to ride bikes. The first bicycle, made of wood with metal wheels, and called, for obvious reasons, a "boneshaker," had been invented in the 1860s. By the late 1800s, steady improvements in the bicycle had resulted in the Pneumatic-Tired Safety Bicycle, which featured rubber tires, metal spokes and gears that allowed the rider greater ease in reaching higher speeds. In the 1890s, the first cycling organization, the League of American Wheelman, was formed and in the 1930s, the low-pressure balloon tire was invented by Ignaz Schwinn who also added straight han-

dle bars to his bikes. During the next 50 years, most manufacturers evolved the old Schwinn bike design into light, sleek
road bikes with skinny tires. And Americans across the country took to paved roads and sidewalks in record numbers.

Decidedly more counter-culture types like Fisher, Kelly,
Breeze and Ritchie held on to the clunkers, however, preferring
to rattle and crash through the trees and over the rocks, down
California mountainsides. In 1976, they held what is thought
to be the first official mountain bike race, the Repack, a 1,300
foot descent Bob Burrowes won (although Fisher still holds the
course record, 4 minutes, 22 seconds, set in 1988). In 1978,
Kelly renamed the clunker, calling it a "mountain bike." During
the next 10 years, as the popularity of mountain biking
increased, a number of modifications were made to the bikes
including derailleurs, better brakes, a more comfortable seat,
much better suspension and a sturdier frame. By the late
1980s, most major bicycle manufacturers were offering their
customers mountain bikes as well as road bikes. By the early
1990s, mountain bikes overtook road bikes in sales. Today, of
the 53 million or so Americans who own a bike, at least 10 million ride off-road at least part of the time.

Even though most mountain biking today is still enjoyed by
recreational bikers and amateur competitors, like most sports,
it is supported by several formal organizations. The major
ones are the International Mountain Biking Association, concerned mostly with trail maintenance and rider safety, and the
National Off Road Biking Association that manages most of the
competition.

The first official Mountain Bike World Championship was
held in Durango, Colorado in 1990 and mountain biking was
designated as a medal sport in the 1996 Olympics.

*   *   *

Since before she can remember, Lisa Sher has liked to do things that put her on the edge. "My mom claims that I was just born a jock," says Lisa. "Even when I was a baby, Mom says every chance I'd get I'd go up and over the side of the crib, just to prove I could do it. She says I was just always going 100 miles an hour."

In school, Lisa was crazy about sports. Because her parents were divorced and her mother was working, she didn't have the proverbial "soccer mom" who could spend full-time taking Lisa to one practice after another. Neither did the family have the money to pay for expensive coaches. That didn't even slow Lisa down. She still managed to play Little League, soccer, lacrosse and hockey. She also became a competitive swimmer and in high school started running to develop fitness for other sports.

But somehow, she always liked riding her bike best. "Even when I was little I liked to ride everywhere," says Lisa. Not surprisingly, just riding was soon not exciting enough. "Mom said that as soon as I could balance the bike on both wheels, I started trying to do all sorts of tricks, always wanting to do something new." Soon she was into BMX competition, tearing up and down dirt hills with the neighborhood boys, always going as fast as she could.

Right before she went off to college, Lisa bought her first mountain bike. "It was a beauty," says Lisa. "It was bright yellow and would really go a lot of places. After I got that bike, I knew I was hooked on that sport."

After graduation Lisa moved from California to Seattle. "That's a great place to live," she says. "It's really beautiful and the people there are really into outdoor things. Unfortunately for riding, there was just too much rain."

Soon, she was back in California. "It's great to be able to practice without getting covered with mud," she says.

Today, thanks to several sponsorships she is able to pursue her passion for biking full-time and even take some post graduate college courses on the side. "My BA is in history," she says, "but I've always really enjoyed art." She's now studying graphic design. "I'm not sure where that's going to take me," she says. "But all of us who do highly competitive sports know that eventually there will have to be life after serious competition."

Although there are a lot of different types of competition that involve a bike, Lisa's sport is mountain biking and her specialty is the downhill. "Mountain bikers enjoy challenging terrain," says Lisa. "That's what mainly separates us from the cyclists who prefer road racing."

Cyclists who compete in triathlons or longer races (the most famous of which is probably the Tour de France) ride bikes made of extremely strong but light materials, use tires that are very light and thin and wear clothing and carry gear that is as light and aerodynamic as possible. The idea is to be able to go as fast as possible on a challenging, but essentially obstacle-free course. A tiny rock on the pavement can often send a cyclist in these races careening into a ditch.

Mountain biking is just the opposite. A mountain bike is designed for the roughest possible terrain. As a result the bike is very sturdy and although the frame may be made of the same titanium and other space-age metals that are used on the lighter racing bikes, the bikes that serious competitors like Lisa ride are also heavy. They have big "nubby" tires and heavy-duty suspensions. Although a recreational mountain biker can get a bike for around $600, competitors like Lisa ride bikes that cost in the thousands.

The courses also couldn't be more different. While world champion cyclists like Lance Armstrong ride on paved roads, mountain bikers—even amateurs—tend to seek out the very roughest and most obstacle-laden terrain they can find. The more tree roots and rocks and bends and dips, the better.

According to Lisa, a competition mountain biking course is even a lot more than that. "Most people couldn't even go slow down the courses we do," she says. "Even though we are experienced competitors we always feel like if we aren't out there on the edge, we really aren't trying."

Being able to ride a bike is one thing. Training for an event like the downhill is quite another. "This sport uses just about every muscle in your body," says Lisa.

Unlike other sports where participants are allowed to choose gear that is designed for their specific body type and weight, all downhill participants—men and women—use the same bikes. Often referred to as "dualy" because both front and back tires are suspended, a competition mountain bike weighs 40 pounds. "That makes a huge difference," says Lisa. "A 40-pound bike for a 200 pound man is just 20 per cent of his weight. A 40-pound bike for a 140-pound woman is nearly 30 per cent of her weight. That means it takes a lot more strength for that woman to horse the bike around."

Hanging on to the bike and steering it down a steep slope requires a lot of what both Jodie Nelson and Lisa refer to as "core" strength. "Every minute you're on that bike you're struggling to keep in balance," says Lisa. "Like surfing, the focus is on maintaining that delicate left to right balance. You have to remain upright when what is under you is constantly changing."

Like surfing, downhill mountain biking also requires both upper body and leg strength. "You may not be on the course for a long time," says Lisa, "but when you're there, you have to give it all you have."

"This is not an endurance sport like, say, a marathon," says Lisa. "It is a sprint. You go all out for a short time. That just requires a different level of fitness. I'd compare what we have to do with what Marian Jones has to do. The people who run marathons may have to be out there for two or three hours, but they don't have to have the same degree of all around fitness that someone like Marian would, who has to put everything she has into it for a couple of minutes."

In downhill mountain biking the person who completes the course first wins. "But this sport is not just about speed," says Lisa. "It's about all-out concentration." Because Lisa is going so fast in such tricky terrain, like Kim McKnight, she must be totally focused every minute. "If you make one little mistake you will be in for a big crash," she says.

According to Lisa, there is no way to really train for the sport except by doing it. "Even though you're going very fast and you're struggling every minute for balance, you have to be able to look ahead enough to read the terrain. You have to be prepared instantly to steer around that rock or bump up over that root. If you can't react instantly to the situation in front of you, you can be up in the air and off the bike in a second."

In addition to practicing, Lisa also works out in gym. "Because what I do is so exhausting, I work out that way. I go from station to station, fatiguing myself, then moving on to the next thing." She also works with a trainer. "I think you need someone to both push you as far as you can go and to monitor your progress," says Lisa. "At this level of competition, I can't afford to be mediocre. I need someone who will make me go to my limits and beyond."

Although in the past, Lisa has had a coach, she doesn't now. "A coach is one thing, a trainer is another," she says. "At this point, I'm pretty confident about my skills as a racer."

Like her sister athletes, Lisa watches her diet carefully. "I'm pretty good about it," she says. "I grew up healthy so I never developed a taste for a lot of unhealthy things like fried foods. I like vegetables and never was big on a lot of meat. I don't even much like cookies or cake, but," she admits, "well, I do sometimes have to have some candy. I really do like a bit of that from time to time."

While some athletes bulk up before competing, Lisa prefers the opposite approach. "I like to feel light on race day," she says. "I generally eat a little hot cereal—probably less than normal. If I get hungry, I eat fruit or an energy drink. I do think it's important to keep your body on an even keel metabolically. You burn a lot of sugar doing a downhill and sometimes I get these odd cravings that don't end until hours later. Then, an almond butter sandwich tastes pretty good."

The courses on which many sports are held vary little from one competition site to another, but this is far from true of downhill mountain bike courses. "They're just all over the place," says Lisa. "In the East, there are lots of trees, roots and foliage. The courses are more like a single track. Here in southern California on a course like Big Bear, the course is dry and sandy and wide open."

If the natural terrain doesn't present enough of a challenge, competition officials add artificial features like jumps. The one unifying feature is that they are very, very hard. "The idea is to keep pushing the riders," says Lisa. "They always make the courses so difficult that 90% of all people couldn't even ride down them.

"The bikes we ride are almost like little motorcycles, only without the motor, of course," says Lisa. "It takes a while to get used to them. The tires are wide and really designed to bump and crunch over whatever is on the course. You could ride them over boulders," she says.

In some competitions, the riders are going basically side by side. In others they start at one-minute intervals. "Still," says Lisa, "you are always racing against the clock."

Even though the bikes have a seat, the riders seldom use them. "You are standing up the whole time," says Lisa. "That's why this sport is so hard on your legs. Your feet are on the pedals and you feel every bump and twist the tires take. Although the idea is to do the course as fast as you can, you can't go full out like you would if your were on a slalom course. You've got all this stuff to go around. You have to go fast in some parts, then slow in others. That's what's so cool about it. There's always something happening all the time."

Because most of the events Lisa participates in are in the mountains, like Kristen Lignell, she has to be very aware of the possibility of altitude sickness. "At Mammoth we start at 11,000 feet," she says, "and Breckenridge is even higher— 13,000 feet. At places like that even the bottom of the course may be at 9,000 feet. In a sport like this you tend to want to always go all-out, but you have to be careful or you can blow yourself up. There's no predicting how your body will react, so you just have to know your body and listen to what it's trying to tell you. One thing I've found to be true, though is that the more physically fit you are, the less affected you will be by the altitude. At least that's the way it is for me."

Still, Lisa tries not to take chances. "If I'd normally do five runs a little lower down, I'll do maybe three if we're really up high. You have to pace yourself."

The bike that Lisa rides is definitely state-of-the-art and has a price tag to match. The retail price would be between $5,000 and $6,000. "The cool thing about it, though," says Lisa, "is that within a year of when we get our bikes, virtually anyone can buy one. We get them first because we're basically the 'crash test dummies.' The sponsors try them out on us because they know that we'll be harder on them than anyone. If something's going to break, we're the ones who will break it. Sometimes what we do to a bike is just not pretty," she adds.

Although a recreational bike owner will probably own a bike for several years at the least, Lisa and the other professionals will go through one in a season. "It's not like we don't take really good care of them," she says. "We get them serviced every week. It's just that we beat them up. But that's what we're supposed to do. The next year, that model will be available for anyone to buy and the manufacturers want all the bugs worked out before they make them for the general public."

Like other professional athletes, Lisa works on contract for her sponsors. In addition to competing and testing equipment, she has other obligations. "You have to do a specific number of rider appearances and a specific number of press appearances," says Lisa. "Then you are expected to meet and mingle with the fans. That's not hard in this sport. A lot of times there are both amateur and pro races held at the same place. So there may be 200 pros and 2,000 other people racing at some level or another.

"I'm good with that," says Lisa. "Part of my deal is that I help sell bikes. So if some fan comes up to me and asks about my bike, I'll say, here, go check it out. Ride it around for awhile. I know that if that guy has a positive experience with me when it comes time to buy a bike, he's going to be more likely to pick the one he got a chance to ride at the event."

Lisa also takes a lot of time with kids. "I give away a lot of jerseys," she says. "If people see this cute kid walking around with this oversized jersey, they're going to remember it more, even than if I'm wearing it. That kid becomes a walking billboard for the sponsor."

This year Lisa will also participate in several riding camps. "This is another sponsor thing," says Lisa. "The people pay to come to the camp—both adults and kids—and learn to ride better. There are always a lot of new bikes there that they can try and if they like them, the sponsor sells them at a discount. It's a great opportunity to get some good advice and also to get on some good equipment."

The camps also have a USA Cycling tie-in. "The kids who participate also get a chance to compete for positions on the junior national team," says Lisa. "There are camps in both the east and the west and the groups will be able to compete with one another."

By participating in the camps, Lisa hopes to reach another goal. "Right now the camps are predominately boys," she says. "I hope that by being there I can attract some more girls."

To encourage more female participation, Lisa also serves as a mentor to some of the junior girls. "I sometimes even let the girls stay with me," she says. "I try to treat them like they're little sisters. I encourage them to try to beat me. I don't think they can, but if they do, I'd be happy for them. I can't say I'd want to do this all the time—it really depends on the girls—but I think it's been a good thing so far."

Since the men's and women's competitions are held simultaneously, Lisa can't help but notice the difference between the way men and women race in the sport. In addition to the advantage the men have by being heavier, Lisa says some of their advantage is basic physiology. "Men just have bigger hearts and can build bigger muscles," she says. "They are also taller and so have a bigger reach. They also don't have to work as hard in the gym to get the same results. That's frustrating. Plus, there's all that testosterone.

"But, women have some advantages, too," she adds. "Certainly part of this sport has to do with maneuvering the bike around sharp corners. By being smaller, women have an easier time with that. We can also sometimes go over rocks easier."

Like many of her sister athletes, Lisa finds that by being at the top of her sport, it is inevitable that she finds herself competing with the men as well. "I could never beat the top five guys, but I could maybe go just as fast as most of the top 30," she says. "In fact, I've been at races where I would have easily qualified for the men's race. I think some of it comes from my background in swimming. Although men are naturally more broad shouldered, I've still got those swimming muscles working for me."

As she gains experience in the sport, Lisa is also more aware of the need to train for injury prevention. "There isn't just one way you can hurt yourself in this sport," she says, "but there are some injuries that can really put you out for a while." While she's gone right ahead and competed with what she calls those "little irritating injuries" like broken fingers and big scrapes and bruises, some things even she can't ignore.

Extreme mountain biking for Lisa Sher is a sport that requires both top physical conditioning and intense focus.

"I was out all last winter with broken ribs," she says. "Initially I thought it was just a dumb little crash, but the next day I fell again and hit the same spot. When eight Advil didn't even make a dent in the pain, I knew something was really wrong."

"When you break ribs you can't do necessary things like breathe," she says. "It's the worst. The other problem is that an injury like broken ribs also cuts down on conditioning. It's hard not to get lazy when you're recovering, but you have to keep at it, even when it hurts.

"I guess I'm just so conditioned to crashing, I don't notice it much anymore," she says. "I'm only aware of the toll it takes when people stare at me like 'who beat her up?' Now it's just so much a part of my life that I forget that going around covered with bruises and scrapes is not what sane, normal people do."

The ribs haven't been the only injury. "I remember back in 1994. The first thing I ever broke was a vertebra. I remember thinking, I'm not Superman after all—bummer."

Eventually the injuries start to add up, but Lisa says you can't let them slow you down. "If you're afraid of getting hurt, you will start riding timid," she says. "Then you won't be competitive."

Like her sister athletes, Lisa believes that a lot of the sport involves mental as well as physical training. "Psychology is huge in any sport," she says. "And I think it's more so in an individual sport like the downhill. Your mind is what limits you in anything—your sport and your life. You will probably always be afraid of some things. But if you work at it, you can manage that fear. Turn it into something positive. I'm going to guess that everyone has a different way of dealing with fear. For myself, I have certain phrases that I repeat if I'm doing a certain thing.

"I know it is corny to say this," says Lisa, "but you really do have to stay focused. You know that somewhere out there, there is someone who is trying just as hard as you are. If you're going to be able to beat them, you have to be more mentally prepared. When I'm about to race, I'm all jazzed up. I have a lot of energy and what I need is to calm down. A more mellow person might need the opposite. She might need someone to fire her up. I try to carry this attitude over into my personal life. If I'm on the freeway and someone is making me mad, I'll try to repeat those phrases to calm myself down."

"Once I get on the course, though, it's like I'm free. I'm having fun. To me it's like playing. I guess that's why all the injuries and the time it takes are worth it.

"Another thing I try to do is not worry so much about the other competitors. It's only natural to be competitive, but you can't think about everything that's happening. You can't even be worried about who's going to cross the finish line first. You have to have a plan. You break down what you're doing into steps and then you get through them one at a time. It's like you have a mental checklist. You say, OK, I did that. And you mentally check it off. If I didn't do that I think I'd probably be all over the place.

"Competition at this level is a crazy thing," says Lisa. "You wouldn't believe what people will do to try and mess with you. I had this teammate who, if I went somewhere, would come over and sit on my bike. I know that seems like a small thing, but when you're trying to get into your ritual, that can really be irritating. I think it's weird that people will do stuff like that. I guess they have to win the easy way. I say, hey, if you want to beat me, come on, let's go race. Let's not do this stupid stuff."

Like most professionals, Lisa has competed all over the world, but this year she'll compete only in North America and in Japan. "If you bring your mechanic along, you're talking about $7,000 a race," she says. "You have to make choices about what you can do."

In the US, the season for competition begins in late May. That doesn't give the competitors much time to practice. "A lot of the places we race are the bigger hills and in the winter they're ski resorts," says Lisa. "Some years they're still snowed in and people are still skiing on them, so you have to do something different."

Depending on the weather, even the usually dry areas may be difficult to navigate. "We race no matter what the weather, though," says Lisa. "If it's muddied up, that makes it a lot harder. It takes a lot out of you. It's a physical sport to begin with and if you have to ride sloppy, it takes even more strength and determination. Mud is a definite handicap. The only positive thing about it is that everyone else has to plow through the mud, too. You just have to put a smile on your face and go for it. It's best if you can just laugh all the way down, even if you're not all that happy."

Muddy courses are often an especial challenge for the women racers. "We usually go first," says Lisa. "So by the time the guys get on the course, we've pretty well cleared it off for them. They won't admit that we've made it easier, though," she adds.

Although she has tried a lot of different sports, she prefers ones that don't have a lot of gear. "I like rock climbing," she says, "but I just can't see carrying all that stuff around. I prefer a sport like biking where you can just get out there and go."

11
Follow Your Own Line

A Profile of Lel Tone—Ski Patroller and Heli-ski Guide

As long as there have been skiers, there have always been those who have wanted to ski the most challenging terrain they could possibly find. For many years, the only way these hearty adventurers could hope to experience the perfect run was to strap their skis on their back, snowshoes on their feet and head up the mountain.

In the 1960s, a Swiss mountain guide from Banff apparently became tired of having to trek for days to find the kind of skiing he wanted and talked a pilot friend into flying him and some of his friends to an abandoned lumber camp in a fixed wing aircraft. The idea caught on and soon hundreds of skiers were discovering the excitement of flying to ski where no one had ever skied before.

While planes could easily get skiers to remote places, the major drawback was that they could only drop them off where there was a runway. It didn't take long for someone to figure out that helicopters would be a far more versatile form of transportation for this new sport and they were soon pressed into service. Their greater maneuverability and ability to land just about anyplace there was a flat piece of land a few yards in diameter, allowed them to drop skiers off in increasingly more challenging terrain. Additionally, the helicopters were able to follow the skiers down the slopes, pick them up and take them back up for another run.

As heli-skiing gained popularity, a string of mountain lodges were built, primarily in Canada and Alaska, to provide housing for the skiers so they could stay in the wilderness for days or weeks at a time. There, heli-ski operators are now granted licenses, which allow them exclusive right to a territory of 1,000 miles or so, assuring that their clients will be virtually alone on the slopes. Heli-ski companies also generally provide a guide, who is not only an excellent skier, but is also a licensed emergency medical technician.

For those who only wanted (or could only afford) a one-day excursion, many ski areas in the US, Canada and some parts of Europe also began to offer heli-ski experiences at out of bounds areas near local ski resorts.

Although there is no requirement that those who participate in the sport be experts, the sport is still pretty much limited those who know what they're doing and are in very good shape. On a good day in Alaska, a skilled skier or snowboarder might expect to get in up to 10 runs totaling more than 20,000 vertical feet. And that, by anybody's standards, is a lot of skiing.

*   *   *

After a blustery cold night of stiff winds that blew another three and a half feet of fresh powder onto the 99-foot base at Squaw Valley Ski Resort, the warm sun finally rises above the mountains rimming Lake Tahoe, sending beams of light shimmering across the steep terrain. As the temperature slowly climbs and the pink and violet sky becomes a cloudless blue, condos and cabins begin to show signs of life. Soon, the lift lines will fill with snowboarders in baggy jeans and skiers in florescent spandex bibs, all hoping to find the perfect line in the new hip-deep, cold smoke powder.

As the spring break holiday skiers and boarders set off for the local coffee house for a hearty breakfast before a day out on the mountain, Lesley "Lel" Tone has already been out on the mountain for several hours. The conditions seem perfect for another fine day of skiing. It's Lel's job to make sure that's the case.

Before it was daylight, Lel had slung her 25-pound pack over her shoulder and hopped deftly aboard the gondola that whisked her and other members of the resort's ski patrol quickly to the top. More snow usually means more fun for the tourists. More snow always means more work for Lel.

"Usually this means getting to the mountain by 6:30 a.m. and skiing my first couple of runs before the sun even comes up," says Lel. "It's generally pretty chilly and the winds can be blowing up to 30 or 40 miles per hour. Our job is to check out all the slide paths, the corridors that snow usually travels down when avalanches occur. To keep ourselves safe, we work in groups of two or three." To assess the snow conditions, the patrollers dig six to eight foot holes to measure the brittleness of the layers to the base.

Although all snow looks pretty much alike to even pretty good skiers, Lel knows from years of experience that every snowfall is just a little different. Some snowfalls make the skiing more interesting. Some make it very dangerous.

On this day, for example, the quick rise in temperature from the night before has made the snow pack unstable. The snow on top of the existing base has landed in a loose and slippery sheet. "It's like when you walk down stairs that have a layer of snow on top of a layer of ice," she says. "When you step on it, the snow simply slips off the ice and you go tumbling down. You have to chip away the brittle stuff before you walk on it. The same is true of snow on the mountain. If we don't dislodge the loose snow before someone skis on it, it can easily become an avalanche."

Halfway to the top of Mt. Emigrant, the gondola jerks to a stop at High Camp and Lel slides her pack over her shoulder again, pulls her goggles down over her eyes and slams the door to the gondola shut behind her. Snapping her blue boots into the bindings of her florescent green skis, courtesy of her sponsor, Nordica, she glides toward the lift that will take her to the Shirley Lake Express where her avalanche control area begins. She and her partner are responsible for Granite Chief Mountain, a particularly steep black diamond run in the mountain's south range. Before anyone else can get out on the run, it's their job to make sure it's safe.

As they traverse the run, Lel notices a broken cornice off to the right. The two of them try to kick the snow with their skis to provoke a minor slide, but when the snow won't budge, Lel takes an ANFO stable explosive encased in emulex gelatin from her pack and places it into the split in the snow. Once she and her partner are at a safe distance from the area, she detonates the explosive, triggering a small avalanche. Creating a small avalanche now will assure that a bigger one won't start later.

That accident averted, they head on down the mountain, setting off small charges here and there, roping off areas where a rock may have been exposed and picking up any loose debris that may have blown onto the trails. In general, they make sure everything is as safe as possible for the hundreds of snow lovers of all skill levels who will soon descend in droves on the area.

What Lel and her fellow ski patrollers do is not guesswork or even just a matter of practice. Each has attended mandatory avalanche courses and every one of them has had to pass rigorous tests to be licensed by the state of California. In addition, they have been highly trained in the use of explosives. "We do everything from placing small hand charges in less dangerous situations to shooting large artillery shells from a truck at the base of the mountain," she says.

Since skiers and snowboarders don't have to pass any skill tests before they take to the slopes, Lel and the other members of the ski patrol have to also be certified emergency medical technicians and wilderness responders. This qualifies them to do revival first aid, perform search and rescue missions and use ropes for high angle rescues in cases when a skier is either lost in an avalanche or is injured while skiing. Lel has even been responsible for training a few of the avalanche search and rescue dogs for the California Ski Patrol.

"Getting a job as a ski patroller resulted from basically two things," says Lel, "being able to ski well and a stint I did as an intern. I was born in Switzerland, and my parents had me on skis when I was two-years-old. I lived there for the first ten years of my life, which is probably why I have such a great passion for skiing."

When she was ten, Lel's family moved to Maine where she lived all through high school. "My school required seniors to write a thesis to graduate," says Lel. "A guy friend and I thought it would be a lot of fun to do an internship as ski instructors for the Sunday River Ski Resort. They ran a month-long work-study program that taught students what was required to be a ski patroller. Afterward, I wrote my thesis about the experience and then, because I had liked it so much, took a year off before college to work on the ski patrol there."

After seven years as a member of the California Ski Patrol, Lel decided to take on another challenge—heli-skiing. "Getting a job as a powder guide depended on two things," says Lel, "my experience and credentials as a ski patroller and who I knew. About three years ago my fiancé Tom's friend was starting a heli-ski operation in Cordova, Alaska. He knew me well and he needed a guide/medical coordinator. Thanks to my experience as a ski patroller and the many licenses I already had, especially my EMT and wilderness responder licenses, I was well qualified for the job. I was put in charge of the safety plans and protocols along with ordering the proper equipment and arranging guide training. The transition from ski patrol to powder guide was really fairly simple."

Lel worked for Pointes North Heli-Adventures in Cordova for a year then joined the Chugach Powder Guides of Girdwood, Alaska in the Chugach Mountains, where she's been on the staff for two years. She serves as a California ski patroller for the first part of the skiing season, then heads for Alaska in late February and stays until the heli-skiing season is over—usually sometime in May or June.

According to Lel, the real difference between her two jobs is that being a powder guide takes her to the next level of skiing. "To be a guide, you have to become very comfortable skiing the very steep, expert terrain you encounter in the backcountry," she says. "There is very little room for mistakes. You are in charge. You have to be ready to act at any moment and in any situation because other people's lives are in your hands. You're responsible not just for making sure the clients avoid a nasty spill, but that they are safe in very tricky terrain. Sometimes that means that, counting your group of four or five, plus the four other groups of four or five clients for each ship (helicopter), there can be upward of eight total groups of four or more people depending on you. Teamwork and communication between guides is crucial for a safe expedition," says Lel. "We are also the first line of medical aid available in case of an emergency."

Because what they do is so potentially dangerous, each year Lel and her fellow guides are required to attend a one- to two-week training program before the season begins. Lel trains at Ruby Mountain under Joe Royer. During the program, she gets a refresher course in all the protocols plus instruction in alpine skiing and the use of ropes on glaciers in rescue situations.

The protocols the guides follow are designated by level. "Level ones are situations that can be handled by the guide staff," says Lel. "An example would be a twisted ankle or knee. Level twos are situations that require some assistance by other guides and a sled or the helicopter to remove the client from the mountain. Level threes are more serious injuries, like broken bones. Level fours are the most serious situations, like when a client gets lost in an avalanche. In these situations other agencies like the state police, a hospital, the ski patrol and the local search and rescue teams usually have to be called in."

In the training program, the guides also dig snow pits, similar to the holes ski patrollers dig to assess the brittleness of the snow base. Powder guides rely less on explosives to control the snow on the mountain than ski patrollers, however, since on the backcountry glaciers there is too much risk of triggering a very large and dangerous avalanche. Instead, they simply avoid areas of the mountain where they feel a real threat exists.

"One nice advantage to being a guide for heli-skiing as opposed to ski patrolling is that the potential for hazard is much more extreme due to the remote locations and the aggressive conditions," says Lel. "Usually this means that the clients are a little more intimidated and a little more cautious. If they are aware of the risks involved, they are also less likely to get overconfident and try the risky maneuvers they might do if they were at the ski resort. So in this way, my job as a powder guide is a lot easier. If they don't get too cocky, the clients are less likely to get injured."

Yet, injuries in extreme backcountry skiing do occur. Last year one of Lel's clients fractured his leg. As his guide, she was the first responder on the scene and was responsible for deciding what course of action would be taken. After radioing dispatch to tell them a level three emergency had occurred, she pulled out her trauma pack and immobilized the leg. Meanwhile the dispatcher notified the other guides and the helicopter and alerted the hospital in Anchorage. Once the helicopter arrived, Lel and the other guides loaded the client into the helicopter and away he went. "We call that a load and go situation," says Lel. That sounds easier than it obviously was. All this took place on a steep, snow-covered mountain.

Although heli-skiing is far more extreme than skiing on a nicely groomed resort run, Lel says that if there is an emergency heli-skiers may get much more immediate attention. "As guides, we can be in contact with local law enforcement or search and rescue teams at a moment's notice," she says. "Plus, because these are our clients, we keep track of them. They don't have a chance to get off on their own for hours at a time like they might at a resort. We also insist that all our clients wear an avalanche beacon. If the skier should get

buried, we could locate him pretty fast." In addition, Lel follows them around with all the first aid gear necessary. "I
even bring along sunscreen," she says.

"The potential for risk or injury is much greater at a resort
because of the sheer number of skiers," says Lel. "In Squaw,
for example, when you have 12,000 skiers of all levels of ability trying to ski the same lines on the slopes, the chance of
them running into each other is pretty great. And the accidents that do happen are usually more severe. They often
involve head injuries or multiple skier accidents and those
can be very nasty. Even though backcountry skiers are on
much more challenging terrain, they have more room to ski
their own lines and, on the whole, they are generally smart
enough to ski within their ability because they realize how far
away from everything they really are.

"The worst accident I've ever seen actually happened the
year I was doing my internship for Sunday River," she says. "I
was the first responder to a fatality. It was a really scary situation. Although I did CPR, I wasn't able to revive him. This,
like most of them, was an accident that didn't need to happen. Skiing really wouldn't be that dangerous if people just
recognized their limits and didn't try things like racing
through the woods or launching off a lip without knowing
what's under it."

The risk for injury is only one of the things that make a
guide's job a stressful one. "As a guide, you're totally responsible for this whole group of people," says Lel. "You're not just
their guide, you're their tour director. You have to not only
make sure your gear is in order, you are responsible for all of
theirs, as well.

"I usually get up around 5:30 a.m. This gives me time to
have my morning coffee, stretch and relax so I'm nice and

Lel Tone spends winters as a member of the California Ski Patrol, springs as an Alaskan Heli-ski guide and summers leading bike tours.

calm by the time we're ready to go. On a normal day, if the weather holds, I'm at the hotel around 7:30 or 8:00 a.m. so I can meet my guests and have them ready to go by 9:00 a.m."

Occasionally, a little baby-sitting is also required. "You need to make sure that everyone is in the right place at the right time so they don't hold up the entire group," she says. "But that's just part of the job. Like any routine, it gets easier the more times you do it. By now, it just seems like second nature to me."

On the first day of skiing, Lel holds a client briefing. "This is particularly important for those who've never tried anything like this before. I take time to reassure them that they are going to be completely safe throughout the week, as long as they listen to me. The more informed the clients are, the more their fear diminishes. For example, if a client is worried that his skiing ability is not advanced enough, I assure him that our first run will be very mellow and that I won't throw him into a situation where he might get over his head. I also let the group know that if at any time they feel uncomfortable, they just have to let me know so I can talk with the other guides. We always try to form the groups based on the skiers' levels of ability."

At he end of each day, every guide attends a meeting at 7:00 p.m. These meetings are designed to help them unwind and achieve some closure for that particular skiing day. "We discuss things like what we could have done differently in a given situation or what happened when a client fell in a par-ticularly bad area. We give each other general feedback as to how the day went."

Not surprisingly, even glamorous and exciting jobs like heli-skiing have their share of paperwork. Every day guides fill out a Guide Daily Form, on which they are supposed to ask or answer questions concerning communications over the radio or the use of rescue equipment. "This is also the time when we do an inventory of the equipment for the next day, so we can be prepared for morning," says Lel. "We may also take this opportunity to move people to different groups so each client will have the most enjoyable experience while skiing with us."

Since a guide job is, after all, also a hospitality job, Lel's day doesn't always end when the clients take off their skis. The job description also includes some concierge jobs like making dinner reservations or arrangements for the guests to go to the movies or a play or take a short trip to nearby cities like Anchorage. The guides aren't necessarily required to go along. "But if they want us to join them, we will," she says. "We help each other out with this part of the job. If I'm really pooped at the end of the day, usually someone will take over my guests.

"On days when a friend covers for me, I usually take an hour or so of personal time," she says. "I take my dog on a very, very long walk or catch up on my e-mail or call my boyfriend when he's in town. On my night off, I usually rent a movie or talk with my roommate or call people back home in Tahoe. It just kind of depends."

Although it probably has its moments, Lel maintains that entertaining clients is one of the most rewarding parts of her job. "It gives you time to really get to know the people you're skiing with and watch them grow, whether it's through their skiing or an emotional catharsis. A lot of times, my guests will really open up to me. I hear about their wives or husbands and their kids. They tell you about their jobs or their hobbies and you really get a feel for what their lives are like beyond the one-week skiing trip. Sometimes, it can be really fascinating, sometimes very sad. It really depends on whether they're up here for a vacation or if they're trying to escape from a bad situation like a divorce or a high-stress job."

Lel says that the rewards of her job are "too numerous to count." She continues, "The number one, biggest gift, though, is being able to make a living doing what I love. And for me that goes hand in hand with being able to work outside. I mean, who else has a better view from their office window than I do? I look out over miles of beautiful glaciers and indescribable views of fresh, sparkling powder. It fills me with gratitude and joy just to be alive and to have the chance to see how beautiful nature really is away from the city crowds and buildings and streets. It's simply amazing. To have the opportunity to free ski in untouched, hip-deep powder every day is a bonus in and of itself, especially when you have an injury-free day where everyone returns safely."

Lel finds that being a female guide is a big plus. Initially, a lot of the men underestimate her ability. But that only lasts until they have skied with her for a few minutes. This year, she is, in fact, the only female guide. "This is a definite advantage," says Lel. "Most men have a tendency to hide their fear from other men. They often find it hard to ask another man questions or tell him they feel uncomfortable before a run. I suppose that's understandable to some extent, but it's potentially very dangerous, especially if one of them gets in over his head and won't admit it. The men find it very easy to open up and confide in me," she says. "It's usually easier for them to let down the macho guy stuff in front of me. Also, I make it clear to them that no question is a bad or stupid question. This usually leaves the door wide open.

"Generally, men don't make an issue of me being a woman," she says. "They look at me as their guide whose ability is equal to all the other guides. When someone does make an issue of it, it's easy for me to isolate the situation because I know it's just that person's own insecurity speaking. I just let them realize their own shortcomings once we're out on the mountain. Usually seeing is believing.

"The other advantage for me," she says, "is one I never realized before. I'm just 5 feet 2 inches tall and weigh 120 pounds. And that's really helpful. In heli-skiing the lighter the group, the better they can fly because other things, like the ship's fuel, must be sacrificed before we take off if there's too much weight. All the pilots love me, because where there are four really big guys in the ship, I don't add much more weight. And, of course, we have more room in the cabin. Really, being small is the best thing you can be when it comes to flying."

Lel also finds that being a female athlete these days really helps attract sponsors. "Companies are more willing to invest in female athletes," says Lel, "especially in extreme sports where the market is still wide open in terms of representation." The opportunity for new and exciting jobs has also increased because more heli-ski company owners are looking for talented female guides to round out their staffs. It's our renaissance, so to speak. I simply can't think of a better time to be a woman athlete. There are so many new doors open in terms of new sports and more talented individuals springing up everywhere. It's really an exciting time."

Like many other women athletes, Lel doesn't limit herself to the sports that provide a livelihood. In May, after heli-ski season is over, she, Kristen Lignell and Jessica Repp will climb Denali. An accomplished cross-country mountain bike racer, she competed in the pro circuit until just a few years ago.

"Becoming more involved as a powder guide forced me to make some sacrifices, so I had to quit racing bikes," says Lel. "I just couldn't devote the time I needed for training since the season begins so soon after heli-skiing." In the off season, she still rides to stay in shape for the ski season, though, leading guided mountain biking trips through the wilderness of California every summer.

Like DeeDee Jonrowe, she also does a lot of trail running. "Last summer I ran the Pacific Crest Trail along with ten other women and twelve dogs," she says. "It was tremendous fun and my dog loved it. Living in Tahoe, you can't help but stay healthy and live an active lifestyle because it's always beautiful and there are so many places to explore."

In the future, Lel plans to be a ski-guide until she decides to be a mother. "That won't be for at least another four or five years," she adds. "I just don't think the two go hand in hand. There is too much risk involved in this type of skiing, especially when a little baby is depending on you for everything. Also, guiding is way too time-consuming when you have a family to think about. It would just split us up too much." She doesn't look at the decision to put off a family as a sacrifice, however. "I have it to look forward to later," she says.

Within a year, Lel also plans to start an entrepreneurial enterprise, an all-women's outdoor expedition company tentatively called Athena Adventures. The first of the adventures will be mountain bike tours. Plans now include a short trip, ranging from a one-day to two-week adventure in the Tahoe and Moab areas. A longer version would be a ten-week tour around New Zealand. She would also like to host seminars that allow women athletes the chance to get to know one another.

"Creating a touring company by women for women has always been a dream of mine," says Lel. "If the mountain bike tours are a success, I want to expand the operation to include heli-skiing expeditions and a big wall climb. Basically, I eventually want to offer any outdoor package that anyone might want."

"Regardless of what happens," says Lel, "I will always lead people into the wilderness to show them the wonderful discoveries to be found in each of us in the world around us. Expeditions have an amazing power to help people realize the beauty that is in each of us. The most important thing in life is to be true to yourself and just strive to be yourself. One thing I have found in my life is that there's always another path. What I've accomplished can be reached in so many different ways. You just have to always follow your own line."

Resources

General Information

Schwager, Tina, Schuerger, Michele, Verdick, Elizabeth. (1999). *Gutsy Girls*. Free Spirit Publishing: Minneapolis, MN.

Rappoport, Ken & Barry Wilner. (2000). *Girls Rule!* Andrews McMeel Publishing: Kansas City, Kansas.

Milestones in Women's Sport
www.caaws.ca/Milestones/milestones.htm

Title IX of the Education Amendments of 1972
www.ed.gov/pubs/TitleIX/part3.html

Outside Magazine
Explore Magazine

Sarah Fisher and Auto Racing

Bentley, Ross. (1998). *Speed Secrets, Professional Race Driving Techniques*. MBI Publishing: Osceloa, WI.

www.indyracingleague.com
www.hickoksports.com
www.sarahfisher.com
http://sportsillustrated.cnn.com

Gretchen Hammarberg and Wakeboarding

www.tommyssurfslalomguitar.com
www.gravitygames.com
www.angelfire.com/co/ramincorp/history.html
www.waterski.about.com
www.jetpilot.com
www.usawaterski.org
www.wakeboard.com

Heather Hedrick and Triathlons

www.nifs.org
http://home.san.rr.com/johnstone/
www.usatriathlon.org
www.trisite.com
www.duathlon.com
www.vrg.org/journal/vj2000sep/2000sepfolate.htm
www.xtri.com

Triathlete Magazine

Lynn Hill and Rock Climbing

Goddard, Dale & Udo, Neumann. (1993). *Performance Rock Climbing.* Stockpole Books: Mechanicsburg, PA.

www.gorp.com
www.womenclimbing.com
www.outsidemag.com/disc/guest/hill/

DeeDee Jonrowe and Dog Sled Racing

Freedman, Lew & Jonrowe, DeeDee. (1995). *Iditarod Dreams.* Epicenter Press: Seattle, WA.

www.cabelasiditarod.com
www.starfishsoftware.com/idog
www.outsidemag.com/events/iditarod98/jonrowe.html
library.thinkquest.org/11313/Iditarod

Kristen Lignell and Mountaineering

Gabbard, Andrea. (1999). *Woman's Guide to Mountaineering.* Ragged Mountain Press: New York, NY.

www.nps.gov
www.mtnguide.com/programs/alpam2.htm

Kim McKnight and the Arctic Man

www.arcticma

Jodie Nelson and Surfing

Surf Flex. Frediani, Paul (2001). Hatherleigh Press: New York.
www.jodienelson.com

Erika Sanborn and Skydiving

www.bpa.org.uk/history.htm
www.michigansuits.com

Lisa Sher and Mountain Biking

International Mountain Bike Association.
Mountain Bike Fact Sheet, International Mountain Bike
Association: Boulder, CO.

www.bmxnonstop.com
www.usacycling.org

Mountain Bike Magazine
Mountain Bike Rider Magazine

Lel Tone and Extreme Skiing

www.adventurehandbook.com
www.purcellhelicopterskiing.com

Powder Magazine

Markels, Alex. "The Land of a Thousand First Descents."
National Geographic Adventure Magazine. Jan./Feb. 2000.
pp. 104-113.